MW00813420

The HANGING of SUSANNA COX

0 11557 00560 8

The HANGING of SUSANNA COX

The True Story of Pennsylvania's Most Notorious Infanticide & the Legend That's Kept It Alive

Patricia Earnest Suter and
Russell and Corinne Earnest
Foreword by Don Yoder

STACKPOLE
BOOKS

Copyright ©2010 by Stackpole Books

Published by
STACKPOLE BOOKS
5067 Ritter Road
Mechanicsburg, PA 17055
www.stackpolebooks.com

All rights reserved, including the right to reproduce this book or portions thereof in any form or by any means, electronic or mechanical, including photocopying, recording, or by any information storage and retrieval system, without permission in writing from the publisher. All inquiries should be addressed to Stackpole Books.

Printed in the United States of America

10 9 8 7 6 5 4 3 2 1

FIRST EDITION

Library of Congress Cataloging-in-Publication Data

Suter, Patricia.
   The hanging of Susanna Cox : the true story of Pennsylvania's most notorious infanticide & the legend that's kept it alive / Patricia Earnest Suter and Russell and Corinne Earnest ; foreword by Don Yoder.
      p. cm.
   Includes bibliographical references.
   ISBN-13: 978-0-8117-0560-8 (hardcover)
   ISBN-10: 0-8117-0560-9 (hardcover)
   1. Filicide—Pennsylvania—Berks County. 2. Cox, Susanna, d. 1809. 3. Unmarried mothers—Pennsylvania—Berks County. 4. Women murderers—Pennsylvania—Berks County. 5. Berks County (Pa.)—History. I. Earnest, Russell D. II. Earnest, Corinne P. III. Title.
   HV6542.S88 2010
   364.152'3092—dc22
         2009049337

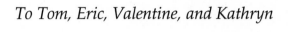

To Tom, Eric, Valentine, and Kathryn

CONTENTS

MAPS

FOREWORD

The story of Susanna Cox is told in a ballad. Americans love ballads. Like their European ancestors, rural or urban, they have always cherished them, from the colonial period to the present, when pop and country singers still feature them on stage, radio, and television. And from the very beginning stages of their adjustments to America, the Pennsylvania Dutch have loved ballads, too. In their southeastern Pennsylvania homeland, their country and town printers issued dozens of ballad texts, some imported from Central Europe or the British Isles, others composed here by local poets. Issued as broadsides—sheets of paper printed on one side—and peddled over the countryside by itinerants or hawked on the streets of the county towns, these songs were eagerly bought and treasured. Often, they were folded and placed in the family Bible or pasted on the inside lid of one's personal dower chest.

According to the usual definition used by folklorists, who have been the most avid collectors and students of ballads in Europe and America, a ballad is a narrative song, one that tells a story. The subject matter of the story line ranges from murder and criminal confession through suicide, unrequited love, gruesome accidents, and sudden death that fell to the lot of innocent members of society.

In High German, the cultural language of the Pennsylvania Dutch for several centuries, a ballad is a *Trauerlied*, or "song of mourning"—in other words, a sad and often touching narrative. The German word *trauern* means "to mourn," and it was even applied in the realm of nature, where English "weeping willow" becomes German *Trauerweide*—the "mourning willow." No wonder that the *Trauerweide* appeared on so many tombstones in the Pennsylvania Dutch Country in the nineteenth century.

While ballads were sung before audiences either in the family farmhouse or on the streets of the county town on market day, they could amuse and entertain, but that was not their ultimate purpose. Heavily moralistic, in keeping with the heaven-and-hell theologies of the eighteenth and nineteenth centuries, their real purpose was to warn the hearers to remain on the "narrow way," according to Matthew's Gospel, and not to venture onto the tempting "broad way" that leads to destruction. In a sense, ballads are weekday sermons in poetic form, much like the medieval *exempla*, moralistic stories incorporated into sermons both to entertain and warn the congregation.

Ballads were normally sung by individuals, rather than groups. For example, they have no choruses or refrains, like group songs, to punctuate the text and rouse the singers between verses. In Pennsylvania, among the Dutch farming population, ballads were often called "grandmother songs," since in the farmhouses the grandmothers were the guardians and transmitters of tradition to the younger generations of the family. They often sang ballads to rapt audiences of little—and not so little—children. We also have the pleasant evidence that some of the grandmothers accompanied their ballad-singing with music they played on the Pennsylvania Dutch zither—a moving and unforgettable scene in the picture gallery of Pennsylvania's folk memory.

Out of the dozens of German-language ballads published as broadsides for the Pennsylvania Dutch by local printers of the eighteenth and nineteenth centuries, "The Sad and Mournful Tale of Susanna Cox," to give its usual English title, heads the list in popularity and numbers of printings. It was sung and treasured all over the Dutch Country, and as well in the Pennsylvania Dutch Diaspora in the South, the Midwest, and Ontario. It was even sung in Pennsylvania High German in the twentieth century, more than forty years ago. In 1961, I was in charge of the seminar stage of the Pennsylvania Dutch Folk Festival at Kutztown, now called the Kutztown Folk Festival. To my great amazement and joy, an eighty-nine-year-old Lehigh County farmwife appeared and sang all thirty-two verses, which I duly recorded. That's a record, since from 1809, when the ballad was written, to the 1960s is a century and a half for the ballad to be remembered in German and sung with the original tune.

Who wrote the German ballads of the Pennsylvania Dutch Country? Most of them, it appears, were written by country school-masters, who set them to hymn tunes they were familiar with, because very often, they served as church choristers (*Foresinger*) or organists as part of their parish schoolmasterly duties. Schoolmas-ters were key players in folk-cultural transmission, not only medi-ating aspects of the elite culture to the common people, but also using, both in their fraktur folk art and their balladry, the people's store of traditional symbolism and its spiritual significance. They were guardians of the community's morals too, instructing their charges at the congregational schools in the principles of right and wrong.

In addition to the schoolmasters as producers of ballads, there were entrepreneurs like the inimitable John George Hohman, who penned the verses, commissioned the broadsides, and peddled over the countryside his popular ballads, along with his even more influential occult medical manual, *Der Lang Verborgene Freund* (*The Long Lost Friend*, 1819–20). The authorship of the Susanna Cox bal-lad is generally attributed to the Berks County schoolmaster, John Philip Gomber (1764–1822), who was connected both with Bern Township and the Kutztown-Coxtown (Fleetwood) area. The attri-bution is not quite settled, however, and for the arguments against it, see the article by Alfred L. Shoemaker in *The Pennsylvania Dutch-man*. The runner-up for authorship is Hohman, also from the area, although his exaggerated ego, which larded his publications with the phrase "I, Hohman," obviously nixed his candidacy, for had he composed the ballad, he would have trumpeted his authorship in every printing of it.

As the authors of this book demonstrate, the Susanna Cox bal-lad went through an amazing number of printings in both German and English. Almost every major printer in eastern and central Pennsylvania issued it and sold it. Occasionally individuals, like C. Erb of York, had copies printed for sale by themselves, and they had their names printed on the broadside—good advertising! One large impressive bilingual edition, the size of a poster, is known.

The authors also have dug deep in the record to tell the real story of Susanna Cox. Certainly the 1809 hanging at Reading, before the largest crowd that ever gathered there, was Pennsylvania's most memorable public execution. The drama and the trauma of it lingered in the memories of all who witnessed it throughout the rest of the nineteenth century, and through written reminiscences, the traumatic event has registered itself even in the twenty-first century.

The reminiscences of Jacob Pile of Amity Township, who as an eleven-year-old boy witnessed the death of Susanna Cox from his parents' covered wagon, are extremely moving. His account was written in 1875 when he was seventy-seven and published in the *Reading Eagle*. I republished it in my discussion of the ballad in *The Pennsylvania German Broadside* (2005).

From the Susanna Cox story we see a rural tragedy involving a hapless hired girl on a Berks County farm who got "in the family way." When her child was born, she allegedly destroyed and hid it and was found out, tried in the county court, and sentenced to death by hanging.

Susanna Cox was not a saint, just probably a rather innocent young woman, caught in the moralistic machinery of Pennsylvania's legal system. And despite the fact that she purportedly had done away with her newborn child, her case has attracted the sympathy of countless Pennsylvanians who learned about it, by hearsay or hearing the ballad sung, throughout two centuries. We trust that this book will continue to produce sympathy for the very human story of Susanna Cox.

Don Yoder

THE KUTZTOWN FOLK FESTIVAL

The Story I'm going to tell you,
Forever will be new,
And who but once doth hear it,
'Twill break his heart in two.

—"A NEW DIRGE CONTAINING THE HISTORY OF SUSANNA COX"

In June 2008, we visited the Kutztown Folk Festival in Berks County, Pennsylvania. This is the oldest folklife festival in America, and it promised many rewards for our journey. The festival began in 1950, when three of America's leading folklife scholars, Don Yoder, Alfred L. Shoemaker, and J. William Frey, organized the event as a celebration of the heritage of the Pennsylvania Germans, often called the Pennsylvania Dutch. Their idea to introduce "outsiders" to the experiences of a Pennsylvania German family encouraged visitors to take part in the festival's events. It was a resounding success, and the festival celebrated its sixtieth anniversary in 2010.

Our excitement must have been contagious, because our family met the idea with enthusiasm. So we packed the van and headed to Kutztown from our home in Delaware.

Looking forward to seeing the crafts made by contemporary artisans in the styles and traditions of our Pennsylvania German ancestors, we drove through Pennsylvania's rolling hills under blue skies that greeted us with the promise of a pleasant day. With building anticipation, we arrived at Kutztown, which even today maintains a homey, small-town atmosphere.

Kutztown was founded in 1755 by George Kutz, who purchased 130 acres from Peter Wentz in what is now Maxatawny Township. It was not until 1779, twenty-four years after the land purchase, that Kutz began laying out plans for a town. Thus, Kutztown was born.

Kutztown sits about seventeen miles northeast of Reading (pronounced "Redding"), the Berks County seat. It is home to Kutztown University, which now houses the Pennsylvania German Cultural Heritage Center. The university and center both offer year-round events and knowledge for those interested in Pennsylvania German heritage, culture, language, arts, and history.

The festival is held at the sprawling Kutztown Fairgrounds, found after snaking through the town behind a seemingly endless line of cars. The event is well organized though, and parking is handled without a hitch. Upon entering the festival, the sights, sounds, and smells are overwhelming. The day is pleasant and as perfect as it can get, especially when considering a sad, but intriguing story that is told to a vast audience throughout the day.

We walked around the festival amazed by the fantastic display of crafts, most of which were made in the Pennsylvania German tradition. In one of the many barns at the fairgrounds, hex signs illuminated a dark corner. Their vibrant patterns were visible from the distant end of the barn. One entire building was filled with incredible quilts, and women worked industriously making even more of them. Booths housed carved furniture, some with rustic charm and others that could grace the finest mansion. Potters, weavers, tinsmiths, candlemakers, glass blowers, and fraktur artists delighted the crowds. Farm-related displays, including the tools of agriculture, covered at least half an acre. Old engines thrummed along, adding to the general noise. Vendors and craftsmen eagerly shared their expertise and skills with the crowds. Questions and curiosity were met with welcoming hands-on demonstrations. A festival is not a festival without food, especially a Pennsylvania German festival. The schnitzel, the roasting ox, the schinken—all were available in abundance within our first few steps into the festival. Visitors to the summer kitchen watch the food as it is cooked. They are welcomed to sample the treats. Fresh bread is baked in a replica of two-hundred-year-old, outdoor stone bake oven. Of course, one needs something sweet after a meal. Viola Miller first introduced Americans to funnel cake more than fifty-eight years ago at the Kutztown Folk Festival. Now Susanne Sharadin continues the tradition. Naturally, all this wonderful food must be washed down with birch beer or fresh lemonade.

There is plenty of entertainment, too. We joined crowds watching Old World dances performed by talented adults and children. We listened to bands playing folk music. And the tall tales are not to be missed. Wandering the fairgrounds exposes patrons to the cultural contributions of the Pennsylvania Germans to America.

Seeking the religious and economic freedoms allowed in colonial Pennsylvania by its proprietor William Penn, the ancestors of the Pennsylvania Germans were German-speaking Europeans who settled in the province in large numbers throughout the eighteenth century. Their contributions through the years are celebrated at the festival. The festival also acknowledges the darker aspects of the culture, including one unfortunate episode that took place early in nineteenth-century Berks County, the hanging of Susanna Cox. Amid the joy at the festival, the laughter of children, and the smiles of indulgent parents, a somber area in an inconspicuous location within the fairgrounds causes sober contemplation. In the 1960s, the event demonstrated in this forlorn area occupied center stage. Now, removed to the back of the fairgrounds, sits the main object of a sad reenactment—a gallows. A hideous contraption, fittingly painted black, the gallows is historically accurate in design, replicated to the exact scale of a real gallows used in nineteenth-century executions.

A coffin sits in front of the gallows. The coffin's simple pine lines make it less noticeable than the stark ugliness of the gallows. To the right of the gallows is a cart and to the left, an Amish funeral hearse. The hearse has no bearing on the history the gallows is intended to relate, but it is fitting within the austere environment in which it is placed. This grim area of the festival serves as a reminder that every few hours, a hanging takes place. Poor Susanna Cox, accused in 1809 of murdering her illegitimate baby, is hanged over and over during the nine days of the festival.

Susanna's story is related to the audience by a charismatic narrator, June DeTurk. It is a familiar story. A beautiful, young indentured servant is lured into temptation and becomes pregnant. The anonymous father is a married man. Alone, afraid of losing her job, Susanna waits through a pregnancy that no one notices and then allegedly kills her baby following its birth. The baby's body is found three days later by Susanna's employer. She admits the baby was hers, but says it was born dead. Susanna is tried, found guilty, and sentenced to hang. After learning that her death sentence will not be commuted, she allegedly confesses to murdering her infant. Less than one month later, she is hanged by her neck until dead or, to use the jargon of the time, "launched into eternity."

June DeTurk borrows a phrase from one of several versions of a much-celebrated ballad concerning Susanna Cox. Printed as a broadside, this circa-1880 version, called "A New Dirge," was published in Pennsylvania by the Neutralist Office in Skippackville, Montgomery County. It ends, "Her exit—infamy!" At the moment these words are uttered to the visitors at the festival, an effigy of Susanna Cox plummets through the trap door of the gallows. It hangs silently for a few moments, allowing the audience to ponder the significance of this event while also providing time for photographs. Even now, although the body is an effigy, this final moment elicits gasps of surprise and shock from the audience. Even little children stop and quietly watch as her body falls, then gyrates at the end of the rope.

One would think Susanna's story is a simple tale in the telling. But this tale is not simple. A larger, more complex story emerges from scant original records. It is the story of a young nation with new ideas, slowly maturing and turning away from Old World cultures and unyielding views concerning justice. It is the tale of the men and women shaping a judicial system unlike any previous judicial system. It is the saga of a simple woman swept along by evolving ideas concerning capital punishment—a young woman whose memory lives in the minds of Pennsylvanians two hundred years after her death. And Susanna's story is a ballad that Pennsylvanians today refer to as the "Sad, Sad Song of Susanna Cox." Her legend is kept alive by the traditions of the Pennsylvania Germans, one of which was to circulate broadsides of ballads. Although the ballad contains the basic outline of the Cox tragedy, its author took poetic license. History is now ready to reexamine the ballad and the event. This is the true story of Susanna Cox.

1

READING AND THE OLEY VALLEY

Susanna Cox, a country-maid,
Young, and of beauty rare,
In Oley as a servant had
Long lived with Jacob Gehr.

—"A NEW DIRGE CONTAINING THE HISTORY OF SUSANNA COX"

A lthough Susanna Cox is hanged annually at Kutztown, that town is not where her saga takes place. Susanna's story begins in the rolling hills of the Oley Valley, a few miles south of Kutztown and east of Reading, which sits in the middle of Berks County. It fell to Reading officials to investigate and try Susanna for her alleged crime.

Separated from the Oley Valley by a hilly region, including Mount Penn, Reading lies along the Schuylkill River, which runs in a southeast direction to Philadelphia. This proximity to the river and Philadelphia allowed for Reading's somewhat modest prominence in the annals of colonial America.

A sprawling, industrial city, the Reading of today is difficult to reconcile with the Reading of Susanna Cox's time. In the early nineteenth century, the sturdy stone structures of the courthouse and jail stood in contrast to smaller, less remarkable log homes and buildings. Gallows Hill, where City Park is now situated, began where Penn Street ended. Today, Penn Street is a wide thorough-

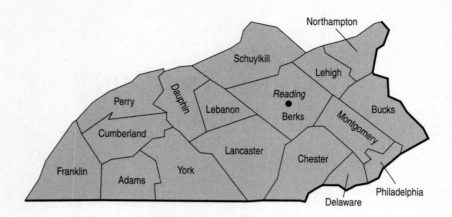

Southeast Pennsylvania

fare, but in 1809, it was a dusty or muddy road depending on the season. While Reading became a hub of activity supplying frontier settlements with arms and other necessities during colonial wars, it was not the bustling midsized city one finds today.

The site of Reading was chosen in 1733 by an English family. In actuality, the Indians used this site as a meeting ground long before the English or Germans settled the area, but they were not the only people to recognize its potential. An early settler named Joseph Finney, a distant relation of the Penn family, lived in the area, which for a time was known as Finney's Ford. Upon his death, it was referred to as Widow Finney's. These names had but the briefest of lives and were to pass quickly into the historian's archives. In 1742, Reading caught the eye of another group of new arrivals, the Pennsylvania Germans, who settled in and around the town. The following year, Thomas Lawrence began to lay out the city. In 1748, Thomas Penn and Richard Penn, William Penn's sons, named the town Reading after their father's county seat in Berkshire, England.

Because of its favorable location, Reading saw its share of service to a growing country. During the French and Indian War, it became a crucial center of defense for an area somewhat protected by the Susquehanna River to the west and a chain of forts along Blue Mountain to the north. Many inhabitants of Reading served in that war, as well as the Revolution. The early iron industry in the vicinity

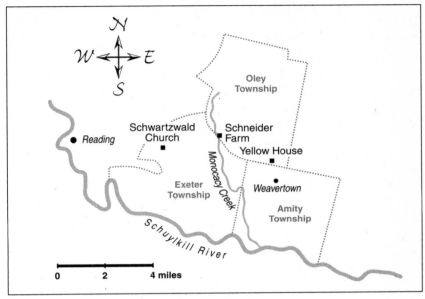

The Oley Valley

of Reading supplied ammunition to Gen. George Washington, and captured Hessian soldiers were imprisoned in and near the city.

Prior to the Revolution, Reading maintained a trade in hats and hides. Later, linen was added to the list of exports. By 1757, the town was home to wheelwrights, joiners, tobacconists, teachers, lawyers, and carpenters, among others. Indentured servants were common; slavery was not. There were nine documented slaves in Reading at this time.

With an increasing population came a burgeoning criminal element. By 1755, Reading had a substantial prison on the corner of Fifth and Washington streets that replaced the previous shoddy, rough-hewn jail. Early on, the residents relied on circuit justices to meet their judicial needs. The town's first permanent lawyer, James Biddle, did not settle there until 1752. A courthouse was erected in 1758 at the behest of the county commissioners, who levied a tax to raise necessary funds. Located on the northeast corner of Fifth and Penn streets, it was completed in 1762.

By the time the Revolution ended, Reading was recognized as one of the more important cities in Pennsylvania. It boasted 417 taxable persons, with a total population of about two thousand. Ninety percent of these inhabitants were German-speaking immigrants, or descendants of German-speaking immigrants. The predominant oral language was a dialect of German, which is still spoken today among some citizens of southeastern Pennsylvania. By the time of the War of 1812, Reading was home to almost four thousand inhabitants. Berks County in its entirety had a population of about twenty-five thousand.

A borough form of government was created in Reading on September 12, 1783. For each administrative office, two persons were nominated by Reading citizens, with the final decision of selecting one falling to Pennsylvania's governor. By 1809, when the Susanna Cox story unfolded, Reading was an established city, a microcosm of a developing nation.

Although many tradesmen resided in Reading, most people in the surrounding area were farmers. Some fared well; others did not. Indentured servitude was common. Not only did indentured servants include those who bonded themselves in service to pay their passage to the New World, but they also came from local families who were unable to care for their children. The Gax family was one of these large, poor families.

The Gax family, known more commonly by their English name Cox, originally settled near Reading in a town known as Coxtown, located in today's Richmond Township. Coxtown was within eleven miles of Reading, but the Cox family soon spread throughout the county. In the early 1800s, many residents of Coxtown lived in log houses on Franklin Street.

Despite having made an auspicious start with a gristmill, hotel, store, tavern, and blacksmith shop, Coxtown was situated in an undesirable place. It was too far off the beaten path and fared poorly for the first part of the nineteenth century. For a few years after Susanna Cox's execution, the town was referred to as Crowtown. Legend has it that this name was derived from a fellow who hunkered in the bottom of a wagon as it rolled through town and "crowed" to show his disgust over the treatment of Susanna Cox. Another name, Helltown, was applied to Coxtown at least once.

In the 1850s, the railroad came to Coxtown, at which point it became more successful. At this juncture, residents changed its name to Fleetwood. It is unknown whether the name changed because of the Cox tragedy, but one has to wonder if the incident had an impact. Two theories persist relating to the name. One holds that the town was named for two surveyors, a Mr. Fleet and a Mr. Wood. Another states the name came about because of a railroad man who was reminded of a beautiful place in England called Fleetwood. Regardless, Fleetwood has been remembered as the town in which the Cox family of Berks County originally resided. It is doubtful, however, that Susanna Cox ever lived there.

Newspaper accounts published long after 1809 report that Susanna Cox's immediate family was large, ignorant, and poor. Susanna Gax, who became known as Susanna Cox, was born to Jost and Catharina Gax on May 20, 1785. In her confession, she stated she was born in Weavertown in Amity Township, east of Reading. Susanna was baptized on June 11, 1785, at Schwarzwald German Reformed Church in Exeter Township, which is nestled in the hills east of Reading. Because of the family's financial circumstances, she was indentured at the age of fourteen to the family of Daniel Schneider (ca. 1747–1804). The Schneiders worked a farm that straddled Monocacy Creek, forming the boundary between today's Oley and Exeter townships, about five miles east of Reading. By indenturing Susanna, the large Cox family had one less mouth to feed.

Because of her social status, Susanna became an "invisible" member of society. She assisted the Schneiders with various unskilled chores. Moving about the house and farm, performing any amount of drudgery, she would not be considered a part of the Schneider family, but she was not entirely separate either. Those to whom she was indentured had control over her life, even the authority to allow her to marry.

Although he based his description on hearsay, the noted historian Louis Richards (1842–1924) described Susanna as having a "vigorous bodily frame, prepossessing countenance and a cheerful and willing disposition." Legend states she was not bright and was considered simple-minded. At the very least, she was uneducated and unworldly.

Reading and the surrounding areas had schools, but they were primarily church schools. For one brief period, Pennsylvania introduced free schools, but by the time Susanna's story begins, those schools all but ceased to exist. Public schools would not begin again in rural Pennsylvania until about 1834. Because children were needed at home and on farms, education beyond the basics was often a luxury. If Susanna was dull-witted, it was probably because she was unable to take advantage of available schools. Even if she was an incredibly intelligent young woman, she was a product of her time. She was expected to sew, cook, and employ herself in womanly duties. Although girls in rural Pennsylvania were often taught to read, many such as Susanna went to work at a young age. It comes as no surprise that, as noted in her confession, she attended school for only three months. This school was probably conducted in the Pennsylvania German dialect.

No available record explains how Susanna became indentured to the Schneiders, but the arrangement could have been brokered through a preacher or perhaps a family friend who knew the Schneiders were in need of domestic help. Regardless, about 1798 or 1799, Susanna went to live with the family.

Daniel Schneider was the son of Jacob Schneider (ca.1720–84) and the grandson of immigrant Hans Schneider (1687–1743). From 1717 to 1734, Hans purchased land in Oley Township. By the time he died in 1743, he and his wife, Catharine Schneider (1688–1774), owned nearly five hundred acres. The house and part of the land on the farm were willed to his oldest son, Jacob. Jacob's brother, Peter Schneider (1723–96), owned an adjacent tract.

Jacob Schneider subsequently willed his homestead to his son, Daniel, to whom Susanna Cox was indentured. In turn, Daniel willed the "old plantation" to his daughter, Esther (1782–1819). By the time her father died in 1804, Esther was the wife of Jacob Geehr (1779–1853).

Indentured servitude usually lasted from three to seven years, so at some point following Daniel Schneider's death in 1804, Susanna's indenture expired. She then became employed by Geehr, whose name is spelled Gehr in some records. The Geehrs remained on the farm, and Susanna, along with her other duties, cared for their young children.

Daniel's widow, Barbara, lived with the Geehrs, but judging from his will, Daniel anticipated discord in the family. Historian Philip E. Pendleton notes that the will specifically directed that Barbara was to reside with Esther and Jacob Geehr and that she was to have "use of all the rooms in the old part of my dwelling house (except the room over the kitchen)." Schneider further stipulated that if the mother and daughter could not "peaceably agree to use the same kitchen and fireplace, then my said daughter shall build . . . another good comfortable kitchen and fireplace for my said wife."

The will was signed in the presence of three Quakers who lived nearby. According to Pendleton, Oley Valley inhabitants occasionally "assembled panels of Quakers from Exeter Meeting to help settle disputes between neighbors or family members."

The Schneider farm was surrounded by neighbors who made significant marks in American history. In 1733, Daniel Boone was born on Monocacy Creek. To this day, the Boone family homestead remains a popular Berks County tourist attraction. Also, the home of Mordecai Lincoln (ca. 1687–1736), the great-great-grandfather of Abraham Lincoln, was nearby. The future president, in fact, was born in Kentucky just two days before Susanna Cox gave birth to her baby on February 14, 1809.

Other Exeter Township residents were key to the Susanna Cox story. These included families named Ritter and Jungman, who established print shops in Reading along with Daniel Schneider's cousins, the children of Peter Schneider. In 1809, these early printers were among the first to publish Susanna's confession and the ballad that captured the imagination of Pennsylvania Germans for generations to come.

In 1809, the Schneider farm had the usual assortment of structures, including a main house, a barn, and an outdoor summer kitchen or washhouse. Because Barbara and Esther may have had problems living under one roof, Pendleton raises the possibility that the washhouse where Susanna's dead baby would be found might have been built about 1804, following Daniel Schneider's death; therefore, it may have been an outdoor kitchen intended for Barbara's use. Summer kitchens separate from the main house, however, were common in Pennsylvania. By baking and cooking away from the main house, summer heat in the family residence became more tolerable.

Louis Richards said the washhouse was built in 1767. He based his date on "a mark" of 1767 found on the small stone structure. That part of the washhouse, the ground-level portion of the building, is now gone. Only the cellar, referred to by some as the "cave," with its door facing Monocacy Creek, remains. By 1809, it appears the washhouse was being used for storage. During Susanna's trial, Jacob Geehr implied in his testimony that the washhouse was also Susanna's "room."

Although records are unclear, Susanna probably lived in the ground-level room of the washhouse. One thing is certain: She had ready access to the structure. Of course, so did others. In fact, on February 17, 1809, Jacob Geehr came to the washhouse.

Early on that cold morning, Geehr needed iron for some household chores. Although not stated in his testimony at the trial, contemporary newspaper accounts claim this iron was to be set aside awaiting the pending arrival of an itinerant blacksmith. In any event, Geehr walked to the washhouse approximately fifty feet from the main house. As he would testify, he dropped to his hands and knees to fish in a hole for the iron. In addition to the iron, he pulled out something unexpected—the coat-wrapped body of a male infant. Surprised, Geehr brought Barbara to the washhouse to show her what he had found. Schneider then "pushed" the body back into the hole. She and Geehr returned to the house, confronted Susanna, and sent a farmhand by the name of Philip Boyer to Reading to summon the coroner.

2

FINGERS OF GUILT

Fear of disgrace prevented her
From making known her state,
Which she by ev'ry means concealed
Despair did indicate.

—"A NEW DIRGE CONTAINING THE HISTORY OF SUSANNA COX"

Because Henry Rieser, the Berks County coroner, was sick, Peter Nagle Sr. came in his stead. A portly man, nearly six feet tall, Nagle was Reading's justice of the peace. He arrived at the Schnei-der-Geehr farm with Dr. John Bodo Otto on the afternoon of February 17, 1809. At the time, the office of coroner was an elected position that required no special training; therefore, nothing was untoward about sending Nagle in place of Rieser.

Those present at the crime scene obviously lacked the extensive training and education medical examiners and forensic experts receive today. Authorities called to an 1809 crime scene, in fact, often added to the problem of solving the crime. Consequently, the clumsy efforts to investigate the scene at the farm amounted to no more than that—clumsy efforts.

The Nagles were a civic-minded family. Two Peter Nagles, father and son, became involved in civic affairs at the same time, making it difficult to distinguish between the two. The senior Nagle was appointed justice of the peace by his friend, Governor Thomas Mifflin. Nagle held this position until his death in 1834. In 1794, he had the honor of hosting George Washington when America's first president visited Reading. Nagle was also one of Reading's few slave owners.

Both senior and junior Nagle served in the Office of the Chief Burgess. Senior became an assistant burgess, while junior became chief burgess. Both Nagles were treasurers for the city of Reading. Peter Nagle Jr. became the innkeeper and eventually owner of the Yellow House Hotel, located on the Oley Line near Weavertown, where Cox was born. While it was probably Peter Nagle Sr., living in Reading, who answered the call on that cold February morning in 1809, either man would have been equally qualified.

Dr. John Bodo Otto (1785–1858) spent his entire life in a medical environment. He was the grandson of the well-known Bodo Otto, who served with Washington as the senior surgeon of the Continental Army when the Revolution began. Bodo was sixty-five-years old at the time the rebellion began, but age was no deterrent to this man, who considered it his duty to serve. Bodo's sons all became doctors. His youngest son, John Augustus Otto, settled in Reading. John Bodo Otto, John Augustus's son, followed in the family's profession. Born in Reading in 1785, his pedigree was impressive. Not only was he a descendent of *the* Bodo Otto, but he was also a Princeton College graduate and read medicine under the incomparable Caspar Wistar of Philadelphia. Otto matriculated from the University of Pennsylvania in Philadelphia in 1808, only one year prior to the death of the Cox infant. At the time of his graduation, many of the great American doctors were professors at the University of Pennsylvania. During Otto's enrollment, he studied with Benjamin Rush, known for his tireless work during the Philadelphia yellow fever epidemic of 1793; Philip Syng Physick, known as the "Father of American Surgery;" William Shippen Jr., a Surgeon General of the Continental Army; and Benjamin Smith Barton, a prominent physician at the Pennsylvania Hospital in Philadelphia.

In 1809, Otto's training was considered among the best. Yet, even as late as the 1870s, medical educational programs provided little of the intense training one receives today. In *The American Plague: The Untold Story of Yellow Fever, the Epidemic That Shaped Our History*, Molly Caldwell Crosby states that by the 1870s, institutions as prestigious as Harvard and Yale still had no qualifying admissions program, few autopsies were performed, and the schools lacked microscopes. But in 1809, all health issues, including those involving crimes, had little value placed on evidence-based medicine. Americans still treated illnesses with lancet bleeding, leeches, castor oil, and arsenic.

As anticipated, differences of opinion emerged as patients failed to respond to various treatments. Caspar Wistar and Benjamin Rush, two of Pennsylvania's finest physicians, had a falling out during the 1793 yellow fever epidemic. Wistar claimed Rush's use of heavy bleeding and purging the infected was inappropriate. While he may have been right, practicing physicians at that time were equipped with a small and woefully inadequate medical arsenal.

The year 1809 was no different. Upon arrival at the farm, the young Dr. Otto, who had little experience, examined the body of the infant. He reported that the lower jaw had been broken and separated, the tongue torn loose and thrust back, and a wad of tow forced into the infant's mouth.

Tow is the shortest of fibers found in hemp, which has a wide range of uses because it is stronger, more absorbent, and more mildew resistant than cotton. In the nineteenth century, it was often used for treating uterine hemorrhaging. Although Otto later qualified his testimony at the trial, his immediate findings would far outweigh Susanna Cox's protestations of innocence.

As Otto investigated the body, Nagle questioned Susanna. Crying, she repeated what she had already told Jacob Geehr and Barbara Schneider. Yes, the baby was hers, but it had been born dead three days prior. None of the evidence in the records indicates that Nagle interviewed residents of the household separately, nor does the evidence suggest Nagle was concerned that the adults confronted Susanna prior to his arrival. Already, in these first moments of investigation by authorities, fingers of guilt pointed without challenge in Susanna's direction. In the absence of properly conducted interviews and forensic science, shadows of the noose descended toward Susanna Cox on the day the body was discovered.

3

MIDDLING STIFF

So far misled this sinner was,
So much bewildered she,
That she her helpless infant's soul
Sent to eternity.

—"A NEW DIRGE CONTAINING THE HISTORY OF SUSANNA COX"

A current definition of *forensic medicine* reads, "application of scientific perspectives and techniques to the legal process, including investigation and courtroom protocol." According to Katherine Ramsland, author of *Beating the Devil's Game: A History of Forensic Science and Criminal Investigation*, most forensic science known in Western civilization developed in the age of Newtonian physics in the nineteenth century.

In 1809, the practice of general medicine was in its infancy, forensic medicine was in its first trimester, and forensic investigation did not exist, at least not in Europe and the Western Hemisphere. The Chinese actually made the earliest strides in forensic investigation. Some of this progress dated as early as the thirteenth century. Advances from Asia, however, had little or no impact on American and European forensics. Instead, European law and procedure, the source of North America's protocol, was taken from procedure that dated back to the Romans. The medical examination was limited to looking at a corpse for outward signs of physical trauma that might indicate foul play.

In Western civilization, progress in forensic medicine was halting at best. Because of language differences and lack of comprehensive and efficient communications systems, knowledge and technological advancements transferred at a snail's pace from one region or country to another. In sixteenth-century Europe, medical personnel in both military and university settings began to study and collect insights into the cause and manner of death. Ambroise Paré, a French army surgeon, evaluated the effects of violent death on internal organs. He also recorded some of Europe's first official criminal autopsies, describing among other things how the lungs of smothered children appeared fluid-filled and speckled with blood.

Changes within the body caused by disease were at this time being studied by two Italian surgeons, Fortunato Fidelis and Paolo Zacchia. Zacchia is considered by some to be the "Father of Forensic Medicine and Social Hygiene."

In the 1600s, compound microscopes contributed to important biological discoveries thanks to Robert Hooke of England and Jan Swammerdam of the Netherlands. It was also in the 1600s that Francesco Redi demonstrated bodies did not spontaneously produce flies, maggots, and beetles. Redi's work proved that the eggs were laid after death. It was not until 1734, however, that René Antoine Ferchault de Réaumur published *A History of Insects*, which according to Ramsland, was a milestone in forensic entomology. This study of insects, as is shown in many of our television criminal and investigative procedural dramas, is important, because the presence of larvae or adult insects can indicate a time of death. The same evidence can also help determine the location of death, if the location is in doubt.

As forensic science advanced, eighteenth-century legal systems struggled to reflect newly understood medical evidence. In 1764, criminology jumped forward with the publication of Cesare Beccaria's *Essay on Crimes and Punishments*. With its more liberal viewpoint, this publication significantly changed how leaders and ordinary citizens viewed criminals, crime, and judicial and penal systems.

The latter half of the eighteenth century ushered in *A Treatise of Forensic Medicine and Public Health*, published by the French physician Francois-Emanuel Fodéré. Europe took yet another giant step forward in forensic medicine, when in 1779 in Germany, Johann Peter Frank published his *Complete System of Police Medicine*.

Despite these scientific publications, it is doubtful Otto, Nagle, or any officials involved in the Cox tragedy had access to or paid much attention to these valuable resources. Otto's education focused more on healing the sick and injured rather than examining bodies for evidence of foul play. Nagle likely gave scant attention to developing advances in criminology, because he probably never anticipated the need.

Yet well before 1809, forensic science assumed a role in criminal investigations. By 1780, Scotland was at the forefront of forensic science and had, in fact, used this science to determine a woman's killer. Such instances, however, proved to be the exception rather than the rule. As in Europe in the eighteenth and early nineteenth centuries, most investigators and court authorities in America relied exclusively on circumstantial evidence, logic, and eyewitness testimony to prove or disprove a crime. These methods did not serve Susanna well.

Regrettably, further advances in forensic science came after Susanna's execution. In 1811, information on rigor mortis was published. It was then that Pierre Nysten published Nysten's Law. He was the first to note the progress of rigidity from the facial muscles to the lower limbs. Nysten documented that after death, the body is lax, then temporarily stiffens for a few hours or days, and then becomes lax again. Armed with this knowledge, forensic experts could determine a time of death. Soon after this discovery, John Davey discovered algor mortis, or the cooling of the body. This knowledge further added to the investigator's arsenal.

While Nagle and Otto mentioned at the trial that the Cox infant was "stiff" or "middling stiff," both appeared to be referring to a condition caused by the cold winter weather as opposed to trying to ascertain the time of death. Neither man introduced into the discussion the relevancy of the stages of rigor mortis. The stiffness of the body seemed only to ascertain the infant was, in fact, dead.

The records remain silent as to what became of the infant's body. It is unlikely Otto removed the body to perform an autopsy. Instead he examined the body *in situ*, or on site, in the washhouse where it was discovered. Probably the body was then transported to its now unknown burial site. Testimony at the trial suggests neither Otto nor Nagle conducted further investigation of the infant's corpse. At this time, autopsies were considered improper. The interior of the body was believed by some to be God's territory and to cut a person open would be intruding into sacred domain.

The unfortunate consequence of lack of further forensic investigation became apparent at Susanna's trial. In their efforts to provide honest testimony, Otto and Dr. John Christian Baum, who testified in defense of Susanna, were faced with the very real problem of lack of scientific data, coupled with public disdain concerning autopsies. Both doctors drew on personal experience, but neither had sufficient scientific knowledge to know whether the baby was born alive or, as Susanna claimed, born dead. They did not even know if the baby, if born alive, had been murdered or died of natural causes.

Today's forensic analysts are able to determine if a baby was stillborn by looking at the infant's lungs. If a breath was drawn, the baby was born alive. This method was used in the recent and well-known Grossberg–Peterson case. Amy Grossberg was the young woman who along with her sweetheart, Brian Peterson, killed their infant son in Newark, Delaware, in 1996. Like Susanna Cox, Grossberg concealed her pregnancy. Upon the birth of the infant, one of the two lovers killed the baby, depositing the tiny body in a dumpster. Both Grossberg and Peterson originally claimed the child was stillborn; an autopsy of the lungs, however, revealed the child had been born alive and had drawn air. Both Peterson and Grossberg were charged with murder.

The point at which medical professionals and investigators began using evidence of air in the lungs as a determinant of live birth remains uncertain. Otto clearly did not have this knowledge at his disposal. Likewise, one cannot pinpoint the time in history that forensic investigation became the norm and not the exception. Its gradual application was barely perceptible in the early decades of the nineteenth century and completely absent in the Cox tragedy.

In 1809, however, a case in Raleigh, North Carolina, involved forensic medicine. Cabinetmaker John Owen was indicted for murder. He was accused of attacking Patrick Conway with malice, having beaten him to death with a pine stick. Owen was found guilty. His attorney appealed, arguing the indictment was faulty in that it did not "set forth the length and depth of the mortal wounds." A majority of the Supreme Court of North Carolina agreed, saying, "wounds capable of description must be described, that the Court may judge whether it be probable, that death might have been produced by them." Since the indictment had not described the wounds, the case was overturned and Owen received a new trial. Meanwhile, the North Carolina legislature swiftly passed an act in 1811 to constrain what they considered excesses in interpreting the law relative to medical evidence.

A mere twenty-four years after the Cox tragedy, evidence gained from autopsies began to be admissible in court. In 1833, Samuel Gross studied medical jurisprudence in Philadelphia. At the time, he resided in Easton, north of Philadelphia, and it was there a pregnant woman was found strangled. The suspect was her lover, a man named Goetter. When he realized he was the prime suspect, Goetter engaged the well-known Philadelphia lawyer, James Madison Porter, to defend him. At the trial, Gross maintained death was caused by strangulation, only to have his testimony challenged by Porter. Porter argued strenuously against Gross, claiming Gross failed to examine the woman's brain for other possible causes of death. Gross testified that his research demonstrated asphyxia as the cause of death, thus successfully making his case against Goetter. Unfortunately, such thorough preparation among expert witnesses was indiscernible at the Cox trial.

Blame for a poorly presented defense at the Cox trial cannot be laid solely at the doorstep of Baum and Otto. During the trial, Otto openly questioned his own testimony, and Baum cited a similar case in which the baby was, in fact, born dead. Greater fault can be found in the conduct of the defense attorneys and jurors who failed to ask obvious questions concerning the handling of the body, improperly conducted interviews, open access to the washhouse, and even the identity of the father, who might be considered a suspect. Sadly, indifference to Susanna's fate seemed to be the prevalent mood at her trial.

In our era, the Cox crime scene investigation would be considered a mockery. Complete lack of restrictions at the scene, repeated handling of the body by professionals and lay persons, improper collection and handling of evidence, unchallenged interviews with people involved, and the absence of forensic analysis preempted a fair trial. Little evidence of any kind, in fact, was produced during the trial. The testimony used to convict Susanna was not clarified for the jury by the defense attorneys or the judge. Moreover, the jury appears to have asked no questions of the counsel, as was normal in trials.

As a consequence, no one suggested possible alternatives for the condition of the infant's body. The tow may have been frozen to the tongue. Otto, who used a tool of some sort to extract the tow from the baby's mouth, could have torn the tongue. No one asked if weather conditions contributed to a break in the jawbone or a separated hinge in the fragile jaw when the tow was forcibly removed. The doctors were unable to determine if the baby was born alive or dead. No attempt was made to ascertain if the infant had, in fact, died of natural causes. The only issue Nagle determined with certainty was the baby was Susanna's, and he learned that bit of information because she willingly confessed to giving birth.

For Nagle and the coroner's jury he had quickly raised in the late afternoon of February 17 to witness the crime-scene investigation, the tow found in the baby's mouth was evidence enough for an arrest. Upon being told she was going to jail, Susanna Cox began to cry.

Records show Otto and Nagle conducted their inquest and investigation at the Schneider-Geehr farm in the dimming hours on that cold winter day. According to his testimony at the trial, Nagle gathered the coroner's jury so he could indict and arrest Susanna. It would have taken time for these men to assemble. It probably took an hour to complete the grisly task of examining the infant's body and that same amount of time for Nagle to question

Geehr and Susanna. Nagle, along with his prisoner, probably left the farm near dusk. Whether Susanna rode to Reading in a wagon or on horseback, she traded the warmth of the farm for a cold and terrifyingly long night's journey. While Otto and Nagle returned to the comfort of their hearths, the frightened and exhausted Susanna had no such luck. She was thrust into the bleak horror of the Reading jail.

4

WHEN LAW AND HUMANITY HAD BUT FAINT CONNECTION

As soon as rumor did at her
Point as a murderess,
Off was she hurried to the jail,
The foul deed to confess.

—"A NEW DIRGE CONTAINING THE HISTORY OF SUSANNA COX"

Susanna Cox spent the remainder of her brief life in jail, which was by all accounts horrible. The stone monstrosity was built in 1755 from necessity. Prior to that date, Reading locked offenders in a poorly constructed wooden building that had been erected two years previously. This small structure, only twenty-five square feet, was soon overflowing with Reading's indigent and criminal characters. When it became obvious more space was needed, construction began on the stone edifice at the corner of Fifth and Washington streets.

The jail was designed with functionality in mind. The sheriff and his family lived in two apartments on the east end of the main building, while the prisoners were placed in four rooms above the sheriff's office on the west. In his 1948 book *Two Centuries of Reading, Pennsylvania*, Raymond W. Albright described a bake oven as well as a dungeon in the basement of the jail. Louis Richards presented a 1910 account of the jail to the Historical Society of Berks County, but made no mention of either a basement or a dungeon.

A yard surrounded by a twenty-foot-tall stone wall gave prisoners relief from their cramped indoor conditions. By 1770, Reading officials found it again necessary to add to the structure, because of overcrowding. The county paid for bedding, clothing, and food and negotiated contracts with the sheriff or jailer for the care of prisoners. If the economy was bad, prisoners' provisions were diminished.

Surprising by today's standards is the lack of cells that separated prisoners by gender. Instead of the long lines of barred cells in contemporary prisons, only four locked rooms or wards separated the criminal element from the sheriff's family and visitors. Because of overcrowding, men and women were thrown into the four wards together, often with no supervision. These appalling conditions were common, and when the economy suffered, matters grew worse, as more room was needed for the growing number of insolvents. In 1809, when Susanna was imprisoned, yet another addition had to be made to the building, because of the number of debtors who were incarcerated. After spending much of her life on the relative emptiness of the Schneider–Geehr farm, the crowded prison was hellish for Susanna.

Twentieth-century reports wishfully suggest that Susanna was allowed to sit with the sheriff's family for meals. This scenario is unlikely. Most prisoners were expected to work for their keep, usually at the same trade in which they were employed prior to imprisonment. It is more likely Susanna worked for Sheriff George Marx and his family in the same occupation in which she was employed by the Geehr family. Her prison activities probably included washing clothes, caring for children, and cooking, duties she performed all her life. Other prisoners in the jail made wrought iron nails. A workshop in the jailyard suggests some prisoners fashioned or repaired household and farm-related implements. Evidence suggests that a garden was kept after 1795. In addition to labor performed within the building itself, some prisoners worked outside the facility; for example, they were required to repair or build city streets.

Those without skills were expected to pick oakum. *Picking oakum* meant pulling apart old ropes. The pieces were sold to shipbuilders or the Navy and subsequently mixed with tar to be used for caulking wooden ships. Picking oakum was hard on the fingers and became slang at the time for getting into sufficient trouble to be penalized with hard labor sentences. Slaves and denizens of poorhouses were also forced to engage in this task.

When prisoners had quiet time, they played cards in their wards. Those who were not chained were allowed freedom within the ward. Unlike now, where meals are served in a mess hall environment, the prisoners of the Reading jail stood in a line in the hallway. The thick door that separated the kitchen from the prisoners was fitted with a space through which food was passed. The prisoners received their allotment of food and presumably ate in their wards, or if fair weather prevailed, within the walled courtyard.

When not at work, prisoners were allowed visitors or they could roam in the jailyard. Aside from Dr. Baum, at least one other person is known to have visited Susanna in her last weeks. Rev. Philip Reinhold Pauli (1742–1815) provided comfort and administered to her soul. More than likely, Susanna's sister, Barbara, wife of Peter Katzenmoyer, visited. Perhaps other family members came as well.

Prisoners sharing the jail with Susanna were not all violent, insane, or criminal. People were locked up at that time for crimes that today seem so minor they are laughable. In a society in which one could be jailed for swearing or for playing ball on Sundays, sentences now appear excessive. Imprisonment for such infractions worsened overcrowded conditions. In addition to cramped living quarters, vermin, filth, disease, and shortage of supplies, prisoners had to deal with the possibility of assault or rape, because of poor supervision. No distinction was made between prisoners based on the severity their crimes, so murderers were thrown together with debtors and Sunday ballplayers.

Life in prison was so horrific, influential persons of the time started paying close attention. In 1786, Benjamin Rush, remembered for his many humanitarian efforts, such as opposition to slavery and capital punishment, penned a pamphlet condemning the use of prisoners for public labor. The pamphlet, *An Enquiry into the Effects of Public Punishment upon Prisoners*, stirred sympathy for prisoners among the general public. A year later, a group of well-known Philadelphians established the Philadelphia Society for

Alleviating the Miseries of Public Prisons. Its goal was to end what members considered illegal, abusive, and appalling conditions for inmates. This group visited prisons throughout Pennsylvania, seeking penal legislation and reform. Early members of the group included such influential notables as the Shippen and Bailey families. The Shippens claimed among them a governor, a wealthy merchant, and civic leaders, as well as the aforementioned Dr. William Shippen Jr. The Baileys were printers who put their lives at risk during the Revolution by publishing broadsides and other materials for the Continental Congress. Charles Evans, one of Cox's defense attorneys, studied law under members of these important families, just as John Bodo Otto studied medicine under some of them. Eventually, in the twentieth century, Negley K. Teeters (1896–1971) became a member of the society. He was a well-known sociologist at Temple University in Philadelphia who used the story of Susanna Cox in many of his articles.

The Philadelphia Society for Alleviating the Miseries of Public Prisons provided relief to prisoners by donating supplies, money, clothing, and bibles. They also provided oversight, which was uncommon at the time. Prison officials themselves had little supervision and the behavior of the sheriffs affected the prisoners. George Marx's predecessor, Conrad Feger, sheriff of Reading from 1805 to 1808, secured a license to sell liquor out of the room adjoining his office. Peter Feger, Conrad's son, acted as both barkeep and jailer. The public, as well as inmates, were allowed to purchase drinks. There is no record to indicate whether Marx or Daniel Kerper, the undersheriff and jailer, continued this practice.

The Pennsylvania Constitution of 1790 provided for the election and eventual appointment of sheriffs. The free men of Berks County submitted to the governor two names, one of which was Marx's, for filling the position. The governor had the final say over whom to appoint, and obviously he chose Marx. Little information is available about Marx. It appears he was a quiet man who took his duties seriously. When his elected period as sheriff ended, he served in the War of 1812. He became a captain and commanded a company at York, Pennsylvania, from August 28, 1814, to March of the following year.

It appears Marx did not travel to the Schneider–Geehr farm to investigate the alleged crime that had taken place there, because this was not his responsibility. His duties encompassed the operation of the jail and peacekeeping within Reading. Also, because Marx's training differed little from that of the coroner or the justice of the peace, there was no real reason for him to visit the farm. Otto's suspicions of murder, as well as the word of Nagle, would have been good enough.

More is known about the undersheriff, Daniel Kerper. He was more politically ambitious than Marx and had served as Reading's coroner from 1803 to 1805. Replacing Marx, Kerper became sheriff in 1812, holding the position for two years and then again in 1824 for another two years. In 1815, he was a member of the Berks County Assembly. Kerper also volunteered for fundraising for the Lutheran Church in Reading. Both Marx and Kerper appear to have been good to Susanna Cox. In her confession, she thanked them for their kind treatment towards her.

The old stone jail was eventually sold in 1849 and became a provisions store. Demolished late in 1910, the lock from one of the doors was gifted to the Historical Society of Berks County. It remains uncertain if the lock secured the door of Susanna's ward, but some claim it was the lock to her "cell."

In 1910, Louis Richards, perhaps in response to the horrors he saw in the Civil War and a hanging he witnessed in 1870, wrote:

It will thus be seen that the old jail, by its sinister associations, constituted a gloomy reminder of the times, now happily long gone by, when law and humanity had but faint connection. Its walls were doubtless witnesses of human suffering beyond the power of mind to conceive or pen to describe. It is well indeed that it has forever disappeared from sight.

These words appropriately describe the environment where the unfortunate Susanna Cox spent her remaining days.

5

TWELVE HONEST MEN

A jury then empanelled was
To investigate her case,
And to decide accordingly
What sentence should take place.

—"A NEW DIRGE CONTAINING THE HISTORY OF SUSANNA COX"

S usanna's first documented foray from the jail occurred on April 7, 1809, the date set for her trial. One report said she wore a brown homespun dress. She was led along Reading's dirt roads to the two-story limestone courthouse on Penn Square. The tall building contained a tower that housed a clock imported from London in 1755 and the Liberty Bell of Berks County. Having rarely been off of the Schneider-Geehr farm, Susanna surely felt anxious and intimidated as she was led to this officious building.

The operations section of the courthouse encompassed a space only forty by fifty feet. Court was held on the first floor of the building. The judge's bench sat at the north end of the brick floor, enclosed by a semicircular railing. The jury box was in the north-west corner. Jurors climbed a stairway in the southeast corner of the courtroom to the three rooms they were assigned to deliberate details presented at trials. The fate of many was decided in these rooms.

During the most sensational cases, courtrooms filled to over-flowing with curious crowds. Because little or no seating was provided for onlookers, people stood to witness the short affairs. The Cox case resulted in one of the most sensational trials Reading had experienced in years.

Susanna was put into a prisoner's dock, so that she could be observed easily by the bystanders. An elevated seat for the court crier allowed him to be heard by the throng. Susanna faced the crowd, the judge, the jurors, and the witnesses alone. For a simple girl, this would have been terrifying. Knowing her life hung in the balance, her fear was undoubtedly palpable.

Later in America, juries of peers consisted of strangers. During Susanna's time, the idea of finding persons unfamiliar with her story was not a concern, and it would have been impractical. In 1809, word spread quickly through print shops, where men congregated to learn the latest news and debate controversial issues. From there, people spread news and gossip throughout taverns, church meetings, social gatherings, and over neighbors' fences.

Theoretically, selected jurors would be impartial, but the likelihood of locating citizens unaware of the rampant rumors concerning the Cox case was nil. Whether biased favorably or unfavorably toward Susanna, finding one person unfamiliar with her case, let alone finding twelve, was impossible. Ultimately, a jury of peers consisted of men from the community of Reading.

It was common practice at this time to maintain a small pool of potential jurors at the ready. Today, we also draw from a pool of eligible people, usually voters, but our pool is much larger. People who work at certain occupations, such as doctors, may be excluded today, but any voter may be considered. In 1809, the sampling of people who served as jurors was made smaller still by the ineligibility of women and racial and ethnic minorities.

Another difference between the nineteenth-century jury selection procedures and those of today is the questioning of potential jurors. Now, questions are asked by judges and attorneys, giving all parties the opportunity to exclude a candidate by instituting the "challenge for cause" argument, in which a potential juror may be dismissed because there is reason to believe the person cannot be fair. Attorneys may also use a limited number of peremptory challenges. In addition, in areas of the country that implement the death penalty, the jury must be "death qualified" to remove those opposed to capital punishment. No such rules applied in Reading during Susanna's time.

Contemporary accounts say Susanna's jury consisted of "twelve honest men." That knowledge probably failed to relieve her anxiety. Ultimately, her opinion of the jury mattered little. She was stuck with them. Judging by existing records, her defense attorneys raised no objection to any of the jurors.

The jury consisted of John Riegel Jr., John Getz, John Schenk, Philip Philbert, Daniel Shaeffer, Adam Schultz, Christopher Sterner, Jasper Yarnell, Leonard Stupp, William Hain, George Stoudt, and Jacob Dotterer. While considered upstanding and honest citizens, the members of the jury were hardly Susanna's peers. They were Revolutionary War heroes, postmasters, civil servants, businessmen, and landowners—not women, indentured servants, and domestic help. Susanna's fate was thrust into the hands of these men.

6

A DISTRACTION FROM GRIM TIDINGS

Although she supplicated hard
To pardon her great sin,
Of murder in the first degree
They guilty brought her in.

—"A NEW DIRGE CONTAINING THE HISTORY OF SUSANNA COX"

Like prisons, trials in the nineteenth century were different affairs than those of today. Although law in America was based on the English model, dissimilarities soon developed following the Revolution, when an understandable mistrust of all things English permeated the culture. Attitudes became decidedly pro-French at first, because of the alliance with France during the war and a mood of solidarity when France's own revolution began. As an extreme reaction to the overthrow of British rule, Delaware, New Jersey, Pennsylvania, and Kentucky passed laws prohibiting the citation of English legal decisions and precedents. The New Jersey law of 1799 emphatically stated the following:

No adjudication, decision, or opinion, made, had, or given, in any court of law or equity in Great Britain [after July 4, 1776] . . . nor any printed or written report or statement thereof, nor any compilation, commentary, digest, lecture, treatise, or other explanation or exposition of the common

law . . . shall be received or read in any court of law or equity
in this state, as law or evidence of the law, or elucidation or
explanation thereof.

At about the same time, Jesse Root of Connecticut advanced his
"republic of bees" concept, that courts of a free country should not
allow themselves to be governed by foreign law. These progressive
ideas resonated throughout the nation. In 1808, for instance, Henry
Clay was stopped in the middle of an argument by the Supreme
Court of Kentucky while reading the opinion of Lord Ellenborough,
a British judge. Later, however, because of the availability of
English-language legal materials and the familiarity with British
customs, English precedent became acceptable once again, although
frequently modified for American use.

Despite rejecting elements of European legal systems in which
justice could be harsh, liberal leanings in the evolving American
judicial system did not help Susanna Cox. The pace of granting
American citizens greater legal power was too slow. But it had
started. In 1789, James Madison introduced the Bill of Rights to the
first Congress as a series of ten amendments to the United States
Constitution. The bill went into effect on December 15, 1791. Three
provisions specifically affected Susanna Cox. The first prohibits the
government from depriving any person of life, liberty, or property
without due process of law. The second ensures that in criminal
cases, an indictment by grand jury for any capital or "infamous"
crime is required. Also provided is a guarantee to a speedy public
trial, with an impartial jury composed of members of the state or
judicial district in which the crime occurred. The Commonwealth of
Pennsylvania, and likewise the town of Reading, met these require-
ments.

Like the laws themselves, courtroom protocol took time to
evolve and is still evolving. As forensic science advances, laws are
modified and courtroom protocol is adjusted to accommodate the
law. All elements are dependent on one another. As forensic medicine barely existed in 1809, courts showed little interest in admission of medical evidence. Nor did they concern themselves with

contamination of evidence or chain of evidence. In the Cox case, despite multiple hands on the infant's body, the evidence involving the corpse was considered neither compromised nor inadmissible.

Furthermore, experts then faced the difficulties of explaining medical procedures to laypersons. Today, there are charts, computer programs, and a host of other audio and visual systems to demonstrate trauma. In 1809, spoken testimony was typically the only means of describing abuses to the body.

Additionally, rules of hearsay were nonexistent in America until about the 1820s. This allowed Jacob Geehr to speak on behalf of his mother-in-law and wife. Had the women been interviewed separately at the crime scene, they might have given conflicting versions of the events or added crucial information that clarified or contradicted the testimony Jacob presented at the trial.

Likewise, other practices in effect today that protect the rights of the accused were absent in courts at that time. The concept of proof beyond a reasonable doubt, by which guilt is determined, did not surface as a standard in criminal cases in America until the mid-nineteenth century. This is why there is no mention of it in the 1789 Bill of Rights. Moreover, a judge's instructions to the jury were only beginning to be regulated in order to prevent a magistrate from dominating or intimidating the jury. From the evidence that exists, the judge at the Cox trial withheld his counsel about her innocence or guilt. Also, in 1809, no proper guidelines governed the questioning of trial witnesses. Instead, jurors simply interrupted testimony to ask questions. In this relaxed environment, crucial questions were often conspicuously absent.

Court rituals were based more on what was best for the state, county, municipality, or persons serving in official capacities rather than for the defendant. By Susanna's time, defense attorneys were just coming into existence. Prior to that, in the colonial period, only the attorney for the king was present.

Because of crowded jail conditions and the difficulty of finding jurors, expedience prevailed. In his book, *The Death Penalty: An American History*, Stuart Banner cites a 1673 case in Virginia, in which a general court tried Richard Thomas and Mary Blades for two separate, unrelated murders and sentenced both of them to death in the course of a single day. Unfortunately for Susanna, courtroom protocols changed little by 1809.

Not unlike today, trials and executions provided a perverse form of entertainment in most societies of Western civilization. For the pedestrian occupants of Reading, a sensational trial would interrupt monotonous routine. Reading did have its share of intermittent excitement over the years. John Penn's visit caused a stir in 1788, followed by the arrival of President George Washington in 1794, when he was on his way west from Philadelphia to put down the Whiskey Rebellion. Many residents were so thrilled to see their beloved president and hero of the Revolution that they crossed the Schuylkill and followed Washington and his contingent of soldiers to Lebanon, a distance of some twenty-five miles.

Louis Richards described several popular amusements in Reading. He wrote that, in 1791, Jacob Graul exhibited a camel "from the wilderness of Arabia" at his tavern. In 1797, Lewis Somnia advertised he would perform a "bear dance." Two years later, Salanca gave a breathtaking performance in Barr's Ballroom for fifty cents per adult and half that per child; paying citizens watched a dog perform tricks, after which Salanca set off an astonishing display of fireworks. In 1808, for twenty-five cents, people gathered to see an eight-year-old elephant at the public house of Daniel Ferger; it was billed as the only elephant in America. Of course, periodic church socials, balls, destructive fires, gossip, accidents, scandals, political events, newly published books, robberies, and acts of vandalism added excitement to the daily grind. Such occasions offered only fleeting moments of discourse, controversy, or amusement, whereas a sensational trial could lead to months of discussion and debate.

Some Reading citizens undoubtedly needed no diversions. In 1809 Reading, the echoes of war still rang in the ears of many, and the more prescient citizens sensed stirrings of troubles yet to come. On March 1, soon after the discovery of the Cox infant's body, America passed an embargo eliminating trade with England and France and forbidding all European imports. Susanna Cox's trial would be a distraction from these grim tidings of yet another impending war.

7

AS INNOCENT AS A CHILD

Ere long she in the court-house was
Arraigned before Judge Spayd,
Where, shedding many scorching tears,
She learned her awful fate.

—"A NEW DIRGE CONTAINING THE HISTORY OF SUSANNA COX"

Few firsthand accounts are available concerning the April 7, 1809, trial of Susanna Cox. The court docket survives, but the original trial records disappeared from the Berks County Court-house late in the twentieth century. In March 1900, however, Louis Richards transcribed the records from the originals, albeit in a handwriting that takes considerable effort to read.

Richards's transcriptions, now at the Historical Society of Berks County, are deemed highly reliable. Newspaper accounts from 1809, in fact, match verbatim brief portions of Richards's notes. For example, the Harrisburg *Dauphin Guardian* printed an article on April 25, containing the same major ingredients found in Richards's transcriptions. Although his assumptions regarding the event are subjective, as presented in his article "Susanna Cox: Her Crime and its Expiation," his transcript of the trial notes appears to be accurate.

Richards recorded key elements of the trial from beginning to end, including the detailed testimonies of the four witnesses. His transcript quotes Jacob Geehr, Peter Nagle Sr., Dr. John Bodo Otto, and Dr. John Christian Baum. To his credit, Richards faithfully captured the flavor of their testimonies. Jacob Geehr, probably the least educated of the four and perhaps more comfortable with the Pennsylvania German dialect than with English, strung brief sentences together with series of "ands." He testified longer than the other witnesses and contradicted himself in some places. Nagle's testimony demonstrated he had a better command of English, but he raised issues that were left unaddressed. Otto appeared somewhat nervous and unsure of himself, whereas Baum was measured and steady.

Baum, who believed Susanna to be "as innocent as a child," related to the jury the only words known to have been spoken by Susanna, probably in dialect and translated by Baum. She implored him, "If I am a poor girl I may be honest." This plea fell on deaf ears when it was repeated in Baum's testimony. The jurors, judge, and defense attorneys apparently disregarded most of Baum's testimony.

Ultimately, Susanna was treated with indifference in a hastily conducted trial. She probably understood little of the proceedings, conducted in English. Because she was of Pennsylvania German descent, the dialect was more than likely her first and only language. No evidence exists of her having the benefit of a translator.

From a twenty-first century perspective, it is difficult to judge how much of a disadvantage the language barrier presented to Susanna. With such a large German-speaking population in southeastern Pennsylvania, the commonwealth often accommodated these citizens with interpreters and by allowing German in court proceedings.

G. Thomas Gates described several instances of German-language courtroom testimonies in a paper he presented to the Lebanon County Historical Society in 1973 called "A History of Hangings for Homicide in Lebanon County." Gates told the story of Nimrod Spattenhoover, a German-speaking immigrant who was tried in Lebanon in 1879 for murder. According to Gates, several witnesses at Spattenhoover's trial testified in German. The Spattenhoover incident was followed quickly by yet another court case. This second trial also took place in Lebanon in 1879. It involved six men, all having blue eyes, who were tried for the murder of Joseph Raber. According to Gates, most testimony at the trial of the "blue-eyed six" was conducted in German and translated into English. Nevertheless, language may have caused problems for defendants. Following his conviction, Spattenhoover remarked that things might have turned out differently had he known English. He was hanged July 3, 1879. Five of the blue-eyed six were also hanged.

Susanna's lack of education did not help matters. She was unable to write her own name. When asked to sign her confession, which was written by an anonymous source in High German, she did so with a simple X. Major developments in the short trial were probably explained to Susanna by her three attorneys, at least one of whom knew English and German, but she was never asked to testify on her own behalf.

Susanna's attorneys probably believed that her insufficient command of English would hurt her case if she testified. They may have felt that because of the tremendous stress she was under in this fight for her life, she would break down and confess on the stand. Perhaps the attorneys considered Susanna too mentally incompetent to testify.

Perhaps it was a gender issue. Judging by Richards's surviving transcriptions of the trial records, Esther Geehr and Barbara Schneider were not questioned in court. Yet, according to his own testimony, Jacob Geehr immediately alerted his mother-in-law about the child's body. Jacob indicated she was the first person after him to handle the body. Had Barbara testified, she may have answered questions about the condition of the infant's body, but Richards's notes suggest she was not interrogated by authorities during the investigation at the crime scene or at the trial. According to most accounts, Esther suffered infirmities, which explains her nonparticipation in the courtroom.

While trials were distractions from routine for the people of Reading, the Cox trial became even more of a spectacle because of the prosecuting attorney, Samuel D. Franks (1784–1830). The flamboyant and popular lawyer was admitted to the bar in 1805 and soon after was appointed the Deputy Attorney General of Reading. In 1809, when Franks occupied center stage in one of the city's most spectacular murder cases, he was twenty-five, only one year older than Susanna Cox.

Franks was the son of Col. Isaac Franks, one of George Washington's staff officers during the Revolution. He was a cousin to Rebecca Franks (1760–1823), a socialite known for her great wit and beauty. His pedigree notwithstanding, Franks was a man possessed of many talents. He was popular throughout the area for his neverending supply of amusing anecdotes and his talent in the art of mimicry. Eventually, he became an appointed judge, but many felt his talents better suited the stage rather than the courtroom. A big man with a "large head and a fine face," his prominent nose and red hair especially stood out. He described himself as the best "red" judge in Pennsylvania, although younger members of the bar twice attempted to have him removed from the bench. He resigned his commission on January 12, 1830, the year he died.

It is small wonder the people of Reading were eager to see Franks in action. His showmanship, however, might have distracted from the seriousness of Susanna's situation. The charges against her left no room for a courtroom clown, so from Susanna's perspective, Franks was a poor choice as a prosecuting attorney. Yet, his is one of the most recognized and haunting statements from the surviving docket records. His sentiment, "Peace be to her," has been frequently quoted in articles and essays about Susanna. This pensive and wishful expression was penned by Franks in the Berks County docket after her execution.

As the trial unfolded, Susanna gradually and unexpectedly gained sympathy from the community. Why not? She was young, pretty, and simple. Moreover, her story developed against the backdrop of changing views about crime and punishment. People in communities throughout America were debating capital punishment and the fairness of American justice. But the subtle rise in sympathy toward Susanna unfortunately coincided with other murders having nothing to do with her. As a result, citizens of southeastern Pennsylvania were forced to confront their wavering attitudes.

According to oral and written tradition, both undoubtedly wrong, somebody in the town gathered enough money to give Susanna a fighting chance in the courtroom. Three of Reading's finest attorneys were at her side, but they probably represented Susanna without pay or only modest compensation. Her defense team consisted of Marks John Biddle, Charles Evans, and Frederick Smith. Whereas Franks's character was the embodiment of youth, energy, charisma, and enthusiasm, the three defense attorneys were experienced and knowledgeable. They were also ineffective.

At forty-four years of age, Marks John Biddle was the oldest of the three. He was admitted to the bar in 1788. Charles Evans gained admission in 1791, followed by Frederick Smith in 1795. Their age, experience, and worldliness should have proved a fine counterpoint to Franks's exuberance. Like him, their pedigrees were exceptional.

Marks John Biddle (1765–1849) was born in Philadelphia. His uncle, Edward Biddle (1738–79), is even now remembered as one of the great statesmen of Pennsylvania. A local representative of the Penn family, Marks John Biddle was instrumental in collecting ground rents for them. In *The Black Moose in Pennsylvania*, Henry Shoemaker refers to Biddle as one of the few gentleman hunters of Pennsylvania. Biddle kept a stable full of stuffed animals he shot, like a museum. In addition, he is listed among Reading merchants in Morton L. Montgomery's 1898 *History of Reading*. Biddle was known for being contentious and having unyielding convictions, coupled with a great force of character. Occasionally, this "force of character" put him at odds with those around him.

Charles Evans (1769–1847), the second of the defense triumvirate, was likewise born in Philadelphia. He was three years younger than Biddle, or forty-one at the time of the Cox trial. His parents were members of the Society of Friends (Quakers). At age twenty, he entered the law offices of the esteemed Benjamin Chew, who was a friend of the Penn family and, at that time, Chief Justice of the Supreme Court of Pennsylvania. Evans worked in Chew's offices for a time before he took the bar exam. After he was admitted, he established himself in Reading, but only lived there for two months out of the year. He also maintained a house in Philadelphia, but eventually moved to Reading permanently. According to Morton L. Montgomery in his 1886 *History of Berks County*, Evans's peers were "lawyers of the severe school, who studied law in the original sources of statutes and reports." Evans would adhere to the letter of the law with exactness. This exactness was even replicated in his mannerisms, for he was known to "walk erect, like a grenadier."

Frederick Smith (1773–1830), whose name is anglicized in most records, was the youngest of the defense team. He was a son of the immigrant Rev. Johann Friederich Schmidt (1746–1812), pastor of St. Michael's Lutheran Church in Philadelphia. It is unclear when Smith anglicized his name, but it became a point of contention with his father. Of the three attorneys, Smith is listed as having a "superior" classical education. A handsome man with a long face and sharp but fine features, he was known to be affable and humorous. His ambition knew no bounds. Smith received a bachelor of arts and eventually his masters from the University of Pennsylvania. When he felt strongly about a cause, he was a tireless worker. In 1802, he spoke before the Pennsylvania Legislature on behalf of Sophia Biddle, the widow of Revolutionary War traitor John Biddle. John Biddle had lived in Reading and held office in the Continental Congress when he defected. Smith stressed the needs of Sophia with such fervency that the legislature returned to her part of her husband's property.

Smith had met Evans at the University of Pennsylvania, and the two became friends. When Mary Ann Smith, Frederick's first daughter, died in June 1799, he was inconsolable, and three years later he wrote his will with Evans as a witness. The will read, "And lastly, I request that my Executrix will have my body interred near to my beloved Daughter Mary Ann." Despite the death of his daughter, Smith's ambition continued unabated. He made political strides in Reading, serving as a member of the state legislature from 1802 to 1803.

In addition to Evans, the Smith family counted the Ottos among their close friends. According to J. Bennett Nolan, author of *The Smith Family of Pennsylvania*, Frederick Smith and his family temporarily lived in the home of Dr. John Augustus Otto, prior to 1801. Surprisingly, in such a tight-knit community, the Smiths did not maintain a friendship with Marks John Biddle, and according to Nolan, the two men often expressed differences of opinion. President Judge John Spayd (1764–1822), who presided over the Cox trial, however, was always welcome in the Smith home.

Although Samuel D. Franks wrote the most oft-quoted words regarding Susanna, Spayd is remembered for the most oft-mentioned actions. While associate judges James Diemer, George Ege, and Benjamin Morris were likely present at the Cox trial, the final sentencing fell to Spayd. He had been appointed to his coveted position in 1806 by Pennsylvania governor Thomas McKean. In this era, judges appointed by the governor could remain in their positions for life, as long as they behaved in a manner in accordance with their duties. Spayd resigned his post only three years into his term, slightly more than a month after the Cox affair.

Little is known about Spayd's early life. He was born in a part of Lancaster County that is in today's Dauphin County. In 1794, he commanded a company of Berks County militia mustered in response to the Whiskey Rebellion. He was admitted to the bar in 1788 and served as a member of the Assembly of Pennsylvania in 1795. With his dark hair, soulful eyes, and hard-working demeanor, he could have his pick of Berks County's finest ladies. As it was, he married Catherine Hiester, daughter of Joseph Hiester, one of Reading's Revolutionary War heroes and a future governor of Pennsylvania. This marriage also made him a relation to the Muhlenberg family. The progenitor of this family was the immigrant, Rev. Henry Melchior Muhlenberg, the highly respected patriarch of the Lutheran Church in America.

Although unaware of it at the time, the three defense attorneys, the charismatic prosecuting attorney, and the president judge were now facing one of the future's best-remembered chapters in Pennsylvania criminal history, and the final chapter in a young woman's life. They had only to follow the letter of the law. But as history now shows, the laws were changing.

8

THE LAST MELANCHOLY RESOURCE

Each one may easily conceive
What her own feelings were
To think, Oh lamentable case!
What end awaited her.

—"A NEW DIRGE CONTAINING THE HISTORY OF SUSANNA COX"

In 1718, murder had been the only capital crime for thirty years. That year, at the urging of the British Crown, the death penalty was to be applied to a broader category of crimes, including manslaughter, rape, highway robbery, maiming, burglary, arson, witchcraft, and sodomy. Later in the eighteenth century, counterfeiting, squatting, and breaking out of prison were added to the ever-growing list of capital crimes. Hiding the death of a child, even if one was not involved in the death, was also determined to be a crime punishable by death.

In colonial America, crime was attributed solely to the accused, regardless of mental or environmental influences. Courts entertained little or no discussion of crimes of necessity or crimes of passion. If you committed the crime, you were at fault and punished, period. Self-defense was one exception to the rule. John Locke's *tabula rasa*, or blank slate, theory, and his other liberal ideologies that were woven into the Declaration of Independence had not yet trickled down into the courts of Berks County. Gradually, degrees of guilt, extenuating circumstances, and other ideas promoting tolerance and fairness would make their way into mainstream thinking and law.

In some ways, early European immigrants to America could not be blamed for their black-and-white views concerning justice. Money was scarce and time was precious. It was cost-effective to simply do away with the criminal rather than ponder his or her motivations during a drawn-out trial. Moreover, America was young and still close to its break from the British Crown, which had established capital punishment as a means to keep control and maintain order in its sovereign states.

The belief that a criminal was a criminal incorporated the idea that every person was capable of committing offenses and even atrocities. It was thought that capital punishment would serve as a deterrent. People would not give into the temptation to commit evil if they could be caught and executed. The *Virginia Gazette* observed that capital punishment was a way of "counterbalancing temptation by Terror, and alarming the Vicious by the Prospect of Misery." The condemned was considered "an Example and Warning, to prevent others from those Courses that lead to so fatal and ignominious a Conclusion—and thus those Men whose *Lives* are no longer of any Use in the World, are made of some Service to it by their Deaths."

The lasting lessons and effects of public execution were obvious. For example, in 1755, two slaves named Mark and Phillis were executed in Charlestown, Massachusetts, for poisoning their master. Years later, in 1798, Paul Revere, describing his famous ride, mentioned passing the spot where Mark was hanged in chains. Obviously, even if it did not necessarily deter future criminals, public execution etched a permanent image in peoples' minds. Forty-three years after Mark's hanging, the event was still remembered by locals.

Early on, capital punishment was not questioned or debated, but was regarded as part of life. By the 1760s, however, laws began to change concerning lesser crimes. By the 1780s and 1790s, capital punishment, no matter what crime was perpetrated, became an extremely controversial issue, as the public gradually tilted toward opposition. By the late eighteenth century, some law enforcement officers made little effort to catch criminals who partook in lesser crimes.

To further alter the public's attitude towards capital punishment, an influential treatise was published in Italy in 1764: Cesare Beccaria's *Essay on Crimes and Punishments*. The work became a catalyst for revolutionary ideas regarding criminals and their punishment. Both George Washington and Thomas Jefferson purchased copies. Jefferson and John Adams publicly praised the work. The treatise became so popular, Philadelphia printers published two editions, one in 1778 and another in 1793. Beccaria was the first known author to postulate the belief that imprisonment was more of a punishment than death. His work also posed the moral question, does one man have the right to judge another man and take his life?

In 1777, Jefferson drafted a bill in Virginia making murder and treason the only two capital offenses. "The Bill for Proportioning Crimes and Punishments in Cases Heretofore Capital" frequently cited Beccaria and maintained that capital punishment "should be the last melancholy resource against those whose existence has become inconsistent with the safety of their fellow citizens." In 1785, after some delay, the bill was presented to the Virginia legislature. At this time, Jefferson was an ambassador in Paris. Unable to promote his bill in person, it did not pass, largely because it lacked a provision for execution of horse thieves. Pennsylvania, however, became the first state to adopt a similar proposal. By 1786, the commonwealth had abolished capital punishment for a variety of crimes, including robbery, burglary, and sodomy. Murderers, as well as those guilty of manslaughter, rape, arson, and counterfeiting, would still be subject to hanging.

About 1793, Pennsylvania governor Thomas Mifflin approached the state's Supreme Court justice William Bradford, a popular Philadelphian, to garner his influence and support in limiting the use of the death penalty. The following year, President Washington appointed Bradford to the cabinet post of Attorney General of the

United States. Along with Jefferson, Bradford was one of the first to distinguish between degrees of murder. He became a staunch supporter of early childhood education as a means to prevent later criminal behavior. He, too, read and often quoted Beccaria. Bradford's popular essay to the legislature, "An Inquiry How Far the Punishment of Death Is Necessary in Pennsylvania," was modeled on Beccaria's work and was influential in limiting the implementation of the death penalty in Pennsylvania. Other states would soon follow.

By 1794, Pennsylvania had established the prison sentence as punishment for criminal offenses, except for murder and treason. The commonwealth had already established its first penitentiary in the 1780s. The penitentiary system is based on the theory that prison should be a place of "penitence," where criminals reflect on their moral choices, acknowledge their crimes, and thus become rehabilitated. The idea remained unpopular because of the continued belief that severe punishment deterred crime, coupled with the protests over the cost of lengthy incarceration. Attitudes began to change toward the end of the eighteenth century, however. In 1798, four other states followed Pennsylvania's lead in establishing penitentiary systems. At almost the same time, murder was being divided into degrees.

First-degree murder, the only class of murder that warranted the death penalty under Pennsylvania law, had to be deliberate, willful, and premeditated. If a murder occurred during the commission of arson, burglary, or rape, it was considered premeditated. All other murders were second degree and punishable by prison time.

To confuse matters, capital punishment did not necessarily lead to the death of the condemned. The courts had at their disposal means of enforcing capital punishment without killing the criminal. Simulated hangings and gallows reprieves were two options officials could enact. In the Cox trial, officials chose to ignore these alternatives. Susanna's case was based on what now would be viewed as circumstantial evidence, so other avenues of punishing her short of execution would have been considered today. By modern standards, her trial was a travesty because of an indifference that persisted at a time when harsh punishments were being reevaluated.

Unlike today, Susanna's youth did not protect her, nor did her apparent simplicity. Many precedents for hanging young offenders were known at the time. A twelve-year-old girl named Hannah Ocuish of Groton, Connecticut, murdered a six-year-old girl with whom she had an argument. Hannah's mother was an alcoholic Pequot Indian and her father an unknown white man. Hannah was apparently disabled mentally and she was passed from one foster home to another. Neither her youth nor her lack of sufficient mental faculties saved her. She was hanged in 1786.

In 1809, temporary insanity as a mitigating factor was unheard of. For instance, in 1812, John Schild, a Berks County farmer, was charged with slaying his parents. On August 12, he went on a murderous rampage. In a bizarre course of events, he urged his father to fetch Rev. Philip Reinhold Pauli to perform the Lord's Supper. When the father left to find Pauli, Schild took an alternate route to Pauli's residence and was informed that Pauli had gone with John's father. At the Schild home, Pauli performed his duty and left, therefore escaping a chilling scene in which he might have become a murder victim himself. When John returned home, seemingly with no provocation, he savagely massacred his family. Armed with an axe, he first attacked his father, delivering a fatal blow. He then quickly dispatched his mother. He even axed the family dog, cutting off its legs. John's wife and children fled the house in terror, seeking refuge in the nearby woods. Then, in his grip of madness, John hacked the furniture to pieces with the bloody axe. His actions had all the appearances of those committed by an insane person, but the idea of insanity was not a consideration at the time. Pleas of temporary insanity would not be used in courts until 1859.

The death penalty was applied without regard to age, gender, mental state, or any other circumstances. Yet, as noted, if these factors were not enough to save Susanna Cox, other forms of punishment were available to the court that could have circumvented her death. In 1677, Elizabeth Rainer allegedly allowed her child to die of neglect. She was sentenced to stand a half hour on the gallows "with a halter about her neck." In other words, she was sentenced to play a part in the ritual of capital punishment without paying the ultimate price. This presumably served two purposes. Not only would she think before neglecting another child, but spectators would also learn a lesson about infanticide. While rare, evidence of simulated hangings was available not only in America, but throughout early modern Europe. In this country, simulated hanging was most commonly used in New England.

Another form of bloodless capital punishment was the gallows reprieve. At the time set for the condemned's execution, the doomed would "walk the long walk." The condemned, the officials presiding over the execution, and the spectators would go through the ritual of a hanging. The preacher read his sermon, the sheriff read the order of execution, and the prisoner said a few last words. The noose was even placed about the condemned person's neck. At the last possible moment, as onlookers held their breath waiting for the final jerk of the rope, the sheriff or another official would deliver a stay of execution. The entire process had the benefit of conveying terror to the doomed, as well as to the audience. The gallows reprieve was also a useful tool in that it showed the kindness and mercy of the courts. Gallows reprieves were short-lived, however. The punishment was decried as cruel and a form of torture.

Another form of punishment was available to authorities in 1809. In 1786, Pennsylvania passed the Wheelbarrow Law. This act made previous death-penalty crimes punishable by years of hard labor. In all, President Judge John Spayd and the jury had options other than death for Susanna. Higher courts defined the law and corrected errors in the system, but the lower courts conducted trials and decided the cases. Consequently, Susanna's life rested in Judge Spayd's hands. Although it was her defense team's duty to propose alternatives to execution, her lawyers did not ask the court for leniency.

Some contemporaries who witnessed the trial or closely watched developments in the Cox case surely felt she was poorly represented. As is true today, a general mistrust of all things lawyer pervaded public life at that time. In 1805, Thomas Paine denounced the "chicanery of law and lawyers." He felt that Pennsylvania courts had "not yet arrived at the dignity of independence." Paine further complained that courts "hobble along by the stilts and crutches of English and antiquated precedents," which were often not democratic, Paine maintained, but "tyrannical." This sentiment against lawyers was especially intense in the lower classes. Members of the lower class often identified lawyers with the upper class. On the other hand, governors were also suspicious of lawyers, fearing their influence and power. The anti-lawyer sentiment was so strong in colonial America that they were actually banned from court in Virginia and Connecticut. In Pennsylvania, it was said, "They have no lawyers. Everyone is to tell his own case or some friend for him. . . .'Tis a happy country."

The gradual shift in attitudes among Americans eventually led to a movement to abolish the death penalty completely. Of course, change comes slowly and not all citizens were willing to abandon the old laws. About 1812, a broadsheet (a broadside printed on both sides) addressed to the Senate and House of Representatives of Pennsylvania by Cumberland County residents voiced concerns about changing laws:

> The usage and custom of almost every nation, seems to prove it an innate universal law, from the savage to the most refined; in which all concur in sentiment and pronounce with one voice this sentence—*the Murderer shall surely die.*

In a rather oddly expressed and gruesome attempt to point out that death was preferable to torture the broadsheet continued:

> The only country now recollected which makes any exception to this rule, is Russia, where, cutting out the Tongue— the grand knout, which strips the victim of his skin and flesh almost to his bones and banishment in this mutilated state, to the frozen regions of Siberia, is so rigourous as nearly to approach in terror to death itself.

Although these Cumberland County citizens and supporters of the death penalty accepted with little resistance the gradation of penalty, total abolishment of the death penalty was too liberal in their view.

Our laws have few steps in the gradations of penalty. They progress, from a fine, or simple imprisonment, or both—to imprisonment at hard labour . . . and lastly Death.

Cumberland County proponents of the death penalty further felt bodily mutilation was a fate worse than death.

To cut off the ears—the hands or feet—or any mutilation, of the person—or torture, are all, contrary to the genius and temper of our government.

Some of the ideologies reflected in the broadsheet still echo the belief that all are capable of heinous crime, and to forego the death penalty would "diminish our abhorrence of the crime." Nevertheless, abolitionists of capital punishment made persuasive arguments, and while the death penalty did not disappear, they made significant strides in changing laws.

Aside from the obvious cruelty associated with execution, the drama surrounding hanging day had unwanted side effects, for the audience began to side with the criminal. The American public often questioned the fairness of trials, the impartiality of judges and juries, the competence of defending attorneys, and whether or not the punishment truly fit the crime.

Especially in a case where many believed insufficient evidence proved the criminal actually committed the crime, crowds frequently sided with the condemned and rallied against authorities. At the same time, public executions lost their effectiveness as deterrents, as crowds grew larger and more unruly. Crimes such as pickpocketing increased. Vandalism became a problem. The number of lawsuits against cities by home and business owners who sustained damaged property because of the unruly mobs attending public executions began to rise. As a result, public hangings became expensive.

As a consequence, Pennsylvania held its last public execution in 1834. Although tickets to witness executions within prison walls were made available throughout the nineteenth century, Susanna Cox was the last woman publicly executed in Pennsylvania. Many credit her tragedy as an influence on the state's move toward conducting executions within prisons. Because of growing sympathy for Susanna Cox, it was not until 1881 that another woman was officially hanged in Pennsylvania—this time within the confines of prison walls.

9

TEN O'CLOCK TO TWO O'CLOCK AND FIFTY MINUTES

He that composed this little song,
In mem'ry of the event,
Was present at the closing scene,
And did the trial attend.

—"A NEW DIRGE CONTAINING THE HISTORY OF SUSANNA COX"

April's Session of Oyer and Terminer ended April 8, 1809. From April 3 through April 6, the court convened daily at ten o'clock in the morning and adjourned at three o'clock in the afternoon. One day was an exception. On Friday, April 7, the day of Susanna Cox's trial, the court adjourned early. Therefore, according to the court agenda, the entire trial, *including* the jury's deliberation, lasted four hours and fifty minutes.

Understandably, the speed with which the trial was conducted raises questions. Although today's standards fit our more complex court system and cannot be applied to the simpler procedures of 1809, the brevity of Susanna's trial troubled writers even in the nineteenth century. Nevertheless, as previously stated, laws and court procedures, as well as attitudes about crime and punishment, were changing throughout the country, but they were changing at an unremarkable pace.

Susanna sat quietly as strangers she did not understand discussed her life and misdeed. The first witness for the commonwealth, however, was not a stranger.

Jacob Geehr took the stand and testified[1]:

On the 17th of last Feby I went into this Room above the Wash House to hunt for an old Iron. I went to the Corner between the Chimney & the side Wall. There is a [opening?] in which is a closet which does not quite go to the floor. Under the closet is a hole. I got down on my knees & reached in & pulled out some Cloth, a piece of old Iron & a piece of an old broken Bucket. I took several things out & took hold of something which was [heavy?]. I pulled it out & saw it was a Child. I intended to take everything out as I knew some Iron was in it. The girls said when they swept the Room to throw old Horse Shoes & Iron in it. I went in the House & told my Mother-in-Law. She p[rayed] in the name of God that can't be. You must be wrong. I told her it was so & she should go & I would show it to her & she went with me & when she saw it she p[rayed to the] Almighty God what is [illegible]. We went back & she went in and asked Susanna Cox if it were her Child & she said it was. My wife asked her if she had done anything to the Child. She said no. My wife asked her if the Child was alive. She said no. Then she asked her if she did not see any signs of life. She said no.

Next, Geehr contradicted himself.

Neither I nor my Mother-in-Law had examined the Child & we concluded it might have been born only have [half] grown. We did not look at it until the jury[2] came. I _____ of the jury & did not examine it.

---

1 Proceedings of the Cox trial come from Louis Richards's transcriptions of the original records.

2 "Jury" here refers to the coroner's jury that Nagle assembled on February 17, 1809, in order to indict Susanna Cox.

The defense allowed Geehr's contradiction to pass. Geehr's statements were probably guided by questions, presumably asked by prosecuting attorney Samuel D. Franks. Anyone on the jury could have asked for clarification on particular points, but they, too, let Geehr's statement pass.

Judging by Richards's transcriptions, the court reporter, Gabriel Hiester Jr. (1779–1831), failed to note who asked questions. As was standard at this point in the history of American court proceedings, documenting comments and discussion at a trial was left to the discretion of the reporter. Some reporters took thorough notes; others made only general comments. No guidelines existed at the time to ensure consistency, thoroughness, or accuracy. Today, complete transcripts are kept and used for reference by the judge, jury, and attorneys. Furthermore, the records are eventually accessible by any interested party, allowing for oversight.

During Geehr's testimony, some indication of coaching by Franks is apparent. Geehr obsessively described how he happened to go to the exact hole where the infant's body was found, a mere three days after the birth. Perhaps the prosecuting attorney was aware jurors might question the coincidence of Geehr rummaging so deeply in that hole that very day. As previously mentioned, contemporary newspaper accounts of the proceedings suggested he was expecting the arrival of a blacksmith, but Richards's notes indicate Geehr never stated so in his testimony. Had the defense and jurors been alert, they might also have questioned why Geehr continued to pull items from the hole, even after he found the iron for which he was searching.

Geehr continued:

I heard Susanna Cox asked that she had put the Child in the hole. I am not positive. I think Squire Nagle asked her the question, but I am not positive. The child was wrapped up in a piece of mans Coat. My wife asked her two or three times the [that] day before the Jury came & told her she would have to tell the Truth & my Mother-in-Law got with her [illegible] tell the Truth but she constantly denied having done anything to the child. It was dead. The Wash House is 6 or 8 steps from the dwelling House. We had no suspicion of her being pregnant that I heard & she [was] never asked [about] her being pregnant. She did not appear as before. Her shape was larger than [it] ever was [illegible] but I understood she complained to my Wife that her courses [menstruation] were stopped. She even [asked?] to apply to my Wife to a Physician for Medicine & she got Some Medicine. The Child was left were [where] we found it until the Jury came. My Mother-in-Law just pushed it back in the hole.

The washhouse is, in fact, about twenty-five steps from the main house as it exists today. To help her conceal the latter part of her pregnancy, in winter months, Susanna would have worn heavy, layered clothing.

Geehr's testimony raised numerous questions that were ignored. First and foremost, Susanna insisted she was innocent. Despite the pressure of being interrogated at the crime scene, she did not falter in her proclamation of innocence. Furthermore, Geehr's statement that his mother-in-law pushed the baby back in the hole should have been challenged in cross-examination. If something as small and delicate as an infant's body, which also may have been frozen, was shoved into a hole for a second time, the tiny corpse might have incurred damage that would compromise interpretation concerning cause of death.

The interrogation of Susanna Cox by Esther Geehr and Barbara Schneider at the crime scene raises the possibility that the two women wanted to rid their household of this distressing event as expediently as possible. Unfortunately, their interrogation, as reported to Nagle, may have led the justice of the peace to conclude prematurely that Susanna was the culprit. Again, because hearsay rules were not in practice at the time, Geehr was testifying on behalf of his wife and mother-in-law. Geehr continued:

The Prisoner was in the Room upstairs of our dwelling House. Was not confined on the 17th of Feby. I [illegible] the

Child. The Jury came late between 2 & 3 in the afternoon about right [night?] like they all came together. Philip Boyer who lives on my land came in to the Coroner. Between 6 & 7 in the morning when I discovered the Child. She told Squire Nagle that she had been deliv[ered] on the 14th. There was no lock on the Door of the Room. Did not know that Susanna Cox had been deliv[ered] on the 14th until I discovered it on the 17th.

At the next stage in the trial, Geehr provided background about Susanna and her relationship to his family. He testified:

The Prisoner lived in my Wife's Family 5 years & has lived with me 6 years—has been in the home 11 years. She behaved well enough or else we would not have kept her so long. A good, quiet, sober girl—were not smart for work & my wife asked if she was not so any good to her children she would not keep her any longer. She was tender & affectionate to my Children. I have two Children alive, one is dead. They have all been born since she lived with me. Last Septr. she got her Medicine & about 4 years ago. She had a stoppage of her Courses & got some Medicine of Dr. Otto & got better.

Richards noted that Geehr said "Dr. Otto" treated Susanna about four years prior for what was presumably a previous pregnancy. He probably confused the names of the two doctors, as he would do later when he concluded John Bodo Otto's testimony. On that occasion, Richards corrected his error. Baum's upcoming testimony confirms that he, Baum, was the doctor who treated Susanna four years earlier. Geehr concluded:

Upon the 14th she complained she was [ill], so my wife told me. The 15th she was up & the 16th and the 17th she was about the House. She generally gets up about day light. The Prisoner [is] about 24 years old. I don't know her age [exactly?]. My wife is sick & does not get up early. On the 14th I got home about night—can't [illegible] how long her complaint but four years ago. She is a single Woman. My family go[es] in her Room every day but we seldom hunt any thing in that hole.

By revisiting the probability Susanna had a previous pregnancy and raising the issue that she was a single woman, Franks was probably leading Geehr, thus setting the stage through Geehr's words that Susanna was immoral. Yet, if his testimony is to be believed, Geehr sympathized with Susanna and may even have been reluctant to implicate her. Otherwise, he would not stress her affection for his children. It is unlikely Franks coached Geehr to speak so positively about Susanna. More likely, the Geehrs genuinely cared for her.

Geehr's testimony produced a timeline for the Cox infant's birth and discovery. His testimony also provided insights into Susanna's life at the Schneider-Geehr farm. But most importantly, Geehr's unsophisticated yet unequivocal testimony was by no means damning.

The next person to take the stand was Reading's justice of the peace, Peter Nagle Sr. His testimony was brief and less detailed than Jacob Geehr's. It also was comparatively smooth, the testimony of one familiar with court proceedings. Nagle began:

On the 17th of Feb'y. ab't 1 O'clock Mr. Boyer called on me and requested me to come to Mr. Gehr as an Infant had been found near His house and the Coroner was sick. I called upon Dr. Otto to go with me [illegible] of them were present. I wanted men over [here?] & young Dr. Otto came here & we got ready & rode pretty fast & got there between 3 & 4 O'clock. Started at [illegible] 3 o'clock & got done in about an hour. No Person ab't the house for [coroner's] Jurors. I commenced an Inquest as quick as possible but it was near night when I got them together. We went to the Wash House & the Child was in a hole under a Closet. I reached in

& drew the Child to the mouth of the hole & directed the Doctor to take hold of it & he laid it on the Window [sill]. I swore [in] the Jury & there [happened?] to be tow.

Nagle next described Otto's investigation of the baby's body. More than likely, no full autopsy of the baby was conducted. In addition to the view that autopsies were improper, the jurists probably felt they had enough proof of foul play after hearing about Otto's examination. Nagle continued:

Tow about its mouth & the Dr. reached in an Instrument & got the Tow out. He cut open his left Cheek, a male Child. I saw the Dr. feel the Jaw Bone. I went up stairs with Mr. Boyer to the Prisoner. I asked her whether the Child was hers & she answered it was. That it was born dead. She said she got it early in the morning of the 14th before Mr. Gehr People were up. I told the old lady to get some warm [illegible] for her & told her to wrap herself warm which she did [illegible] & appeared quite willing to come up. She cried a little when first I told her but was quite willing to come. She told me who was the father of the Child who was a married man. The Child was middling stiff but not so much as I expected from the weather. She [illegible] acknowledged it was her Child but [illegible] it was born dead. The Child had small nails just as children usually have.

Like Geehr's testimony, Nagle's was hardly damning. When questioned by Nagle at the crime scene, Susanna still maintained her innocence claiming the child was stillborn. Importantly, Nagle admitted that Susanna disclosed the name of the father to him. Yet, there is no evidence that any of the jurists pressured Nagle to release his name. In the Berks County court records from 1808 to 1810, no documentation exists regarding the father of the Cox baby. Two hundred years later, the father's name is pure conjecture.

Oddly, none of the "jurors," or crime scene witnesses, Nagle gathered, other than Otto, are known to have testified in court. Otto himself was next on the stand.

The Cox trial appears to have been Dr. John Bodo Otto's first involvement in a criminal case. The same age as Susanna Cox, he was understandably nervous, accounting for his halting delivery. He was painfully honest about his lack of knowledge, which cannot be attributed solely to his youth and inexperience, but to the level of general medicine and forensic science known at the time. Given their negligible or lackluster statements to the court, the defense apparently failed to challenge, or notice, Otto's uncertainty. Yet Otto questioned himself in testimony, further highlighting the failures of the court. He stated:

> On the 17th of last Feb'y. I was requested by Squire Nagle & after we arrived I found it was a male Child from its app[earance]. I supposed it to be full grown [fully developed]. I observed some [illegible] fibre of tow sticking out of its mouth. I opened the lips & pulled it out.

It is unclear from Otto's next statement what he was looking for when he cut into the infant's flesh. He may have been responsible for bone and tissue damage as he handled the delicate body. Neither the jury nor the defense appeared curious, however, about his procedure. Otto continued:

> I divided the upper from the lower Jaw by incision & observed that the lower Jaw Bone was broken & the tongue torn loose from the roof of its mouth and pushed back a little. [It] appeared that the Tongue was thrust back by the Tow. The jaw Bone was separated.

Subsequent articles about the Cox trial indicate the infant's tongue was "torn loose." This is misleading. Otto stated the tongue was torn loose from the "roof of its mouth," but obviously tongues are not attached to that part of the mouth. Likely, he meant the tongue was frozen to the roof of the mouth and was released from this position when he removed the tow. Otto described the jawbone first as "broken" and later, "separated." History will never know if Otto contradicted his testimony or was attempting to correct it.

Worse, the jury and defense team did not ask for clarification. It is possible both injuries were present.

A dislocated jaw means the lower jaw shifted from its normal position at one or both temporomandibular joints, which connect the jawbone to the skull. A broken jaw, on the other hand, consists of a fracture in the jawbone. A dislocated jaw can appear as if the jawbone is broken, and one of the many complications of a dislocated jaw is bleeding in the throat. Another is difficulty breathing. While these inconsistencies in testimony are inconclusive for proving innocence or guilt, the defense could have used them to their advantage. They did not. Otto continued:

> The child had [illegible] app[earance] as children generally have. The Child app[eared] [perfect?] & fully grown [fully developed]. There was some coagulated blood in the mouth. A small portion of [illegible] but in the tow [illegible] can't be positive That it had as much, but as Infants generally have. It appeared to me that the Child had been born alive [but] can't be positive. Will the blood of [a] dead Person coagulate? I am inclined to think it will but am not positive. The Child was frozen, not very stiff. It had a small portion of hair. I am not certain with what [illegible] the nails. Did not observe any blood in the Ears. The body was bloody. I can't say whether the blood was on child by what Dr. Baum mentioned.

With his last declaration, Otto, following Baum's lead, may have been trying to differentiate between blood from the birth and blood from an injury. Had the placenta torn, the body would be bloody as Otto reported. He did not state, nor did the defense team speculate, how any trauma had occurred. Otto clearly stated, however, that he could not be positive the infant was born alive. Susanna's defense attorneys once again missed an opportunity by ignoring Otto's unmistakable ambiguity.

Surprisingly, Otto appears to have consulted with Baum prior to the trial concerning the condition of the body. Baum may have directed Otto to recollect if he saw any blood in the ears and nose,

for these signs of head trauma might indicate a deliberate or accidental blow. No one at the time found anything irregular about the
doctors, one for the defense and one for the prosecution, conferring
before the trial.

Once again, Susanna's attorneys appear disengaged, for they
failed to point out that Otto was so inexperienced he had to rely at
least in part on Baum. Biddle, Evans, and Smith also failed to high-
light that injuries to the infant could have been sustained acciden-
tally during birth, when for instance, the child might have been
ejected forcibly from the womb to the floor or another hard surface.

Incredibly, during Baum's testimony for the defense, someone
asked Baum about judging the age of a child by its hair and nails.
Yet, nowhere in the records is there hard evidence that Baum ever
examined the infant's body. Baum would have relied solely on
what Otto related to him. Baum's experience compared to Otto's
inexperience made barely a ripple in terms of the testimony.

Records suggest the only authorities who saw the infant's body
and testified at the trial were Nagle and Otto. Nagle was a layper-
son and could not provide medical testimony, leaving the young
Otto to inform others of his findings and opinions. Otto openly
acknowledged he based his findings on inadequate forensic science. Moreover, he relayed his admittedly shaky conclusions to a
jury consisting of a group of men who were far less experienced in
these matters than he was. As much as he tried, Otto was a poor
expert witness indeed. Yet his testimony was accepted without
question.

Following Otto's testimony, the court transcript reads, "Mr.
Smith opened on the part of the prisoner." Dr. John Christian Baum
delivered the only testimony known to have been given directly on
behalf of Susanna Cox.

Susanna's lawyers presented a minimal defense. They never
even cross-examined the witnesses, nor did they challenge the
prosecution's lack of real proof. In his article "Susanna Cox: Her
Crime and its Expiation," Louis Richards concluded that defense
attorney Marks John Biddle believed that the facts "developed were

as already been stated." Biddle's name does not even appear in the trial notes recorded by Richards, suggesting he played an especially minimal role.

The defense's conduct is difficult to understand. The very real possibility exists that they felt Susanna was guilty. This could explain why they avoided putting her on the stand. Perhaps they decided to use the missing witness rule, avoiding her testimony because it would be unfavorable to her defense. Another reason for the attorneys' failure to put her on the stand may have been the language barrier; she would have needed an interpreter. Regardless of their reasoning, no tangible defense was presented on Susanna's behalf.

What makes this feeble attempt at defending Susanna even more inexcusable is that the prosecution's case against her was less than vigorous. The witnesses for the prosecution were hesitant, uncertain, and even contradicted their own testimonies. At one point, Jacob Geehr seemed sympathetic toward Susanna. Dr. Otto cast doubt about his own abilities by admitting to his lack of scientific knowledge. And Peter Nagle's testimony opened gaping holes of opportunity for cross-examination concerning evidence gathering at the crime scene and the identity of the father who could be viewed as a suspect. Susanna's attorneys seemed to dismiss the entire affair as if her guilt already had been established, or because she was unimportant—a simple domestic servant whose social status made her invisible. Subsequently, the defense team introduced only one witness, Dr. John Christian Baum.

Baum was the founder of Baumstown, originally called Exetertown. In 1795, the original landowner, William Whitman, laid out Exetertown, and early in his enterprise, he sold few lots. Around the turn of the century, he sold the remaining lots to Baum, who lived and practiced medicine in Baumstown for the rest of his life.

Baum was the Geehr family's physician. History looks kindly on him, because the compassionate Baum seemed truly interested in fairness. His generally favorable testimony about Susanna Cox acknowledged his inability to determine with certainty whether her infant was born alive or dead. Like Otto, he was aware of the limitations of 1809 medicine and stressed this in his testimony. Aside from Geehr, Baum was the only person to testify who knew Susanna prior to her arrest. He probably had guessed before February 14 that Susanna was pregnant, because the first part of his testimony addresses circumstances involving a pregnancy. Baum also heard and relayed to future generations the only words known to be uttered by Susanna: "If I am a poor girl I may be honest." Like Geehr, Baum spoke on behalf of Esther Geehr and Barbara Schneider. Smith opened on the part of the prisoner and Baum related the following:

> I was attending Mrs. Gehr & she told me that she [Susanna] had been sick again as she was 4 years ago & asked me if I would have [give] her something which would be good for her. She explained [when] she came to me that she was swelled some what & had an obstruction of the [bowels?] & hoped I could give her something. I told her I had no medicine with me but as Mrs. [Mr.?] Gehr was to come over in a few days I would hand it over. I asked Mrs. Gehr & her mother if they [illegible] Something else might be the matter with the girl. The old lady laughed as she did not think any such thing as the girl kept on working but she was in the Kitchen & I might examine her. I went into the Kitchen [illegible] to her and said I wished to know if anything else was the matter with her. I told her not to be afraid or bashful. She held down her head & seemed to take it hard, [and] asked if I am a poor girl I may be honest.

Baum then turned his attention to events following February 14, after the baby was born, implying that the cause of the infant's death might have been accidental. Perhaps Baum felt the injuries the body displayed, as described to him, could be explained by a difficult birth. He continued:

> I sent some medicine by Mr. Gehr and was told she had taken some of it [illegible]. For some time after [illegible] the accident had happened. I then went over as it was urgent of

Mrs. Gehr who was very poorly. I was told that Susannah had taken very little of the medicine & the [rest?] was thrown out.

The next passage is revealing. In it, Baum describes his visit to Susanna in jail. No other person alluded to visiting her. Baum said when he saw her, she remained consistent in her account of what happened, even when speaking to a trusted confidant. She told Baum she was the baby's mother, but she stopped short of confessing to murder. Baum said, "I went up the next day to Jail. She cried & confessed that she was the mother of the Child. P[ray] she was as innocent as a Child." Baum suggested Susanna did not mention her pregnancy to the Geehrs, because according to his testimony, "the weather was bad & it [she] would have been frightened Mrs. Gehr & they would have turned her out."

Baum was interrupted at this point by a question posed perhaps by Smith. He was asked if he knew of other cases in which the woman presumably had the same symptoms. Baum told of being consulted by a married woman who also appeared to have an obstruction. The woman's mother was the midwife who tended the woman, but when "they" thought she was dying, they sent for Baum. Next Baum, with one of the defense attorneys leading him, briefly discussed two possible scenarios regarding the Cox baby's death: the medicine might have debilitated the child and the infant may have incurred injuries during birth. They were suggesting that the umbilical cord had possibly wrapped around the baby's neck. Baum said, "I think if a child had been choked it would have affected him in this manor [manner]."

Baum then delivered one last crucial piece of testimony.

Children of 7 & 8 months have hair and nails. Of the after Birth [illegible] the childs mouth is generally filled with blood and it will coagulate when the child gets cold. Children born in this way are generally dead.

Given the seriousness of Baum's last statement, Susanna's defense attorneys should have repeated this statement time and again, thereby firmly planting doubt in the jurors' minds. Normally, defense attorneys, alert for such openings, would press for clarification about the probability of a stillbirth. Instead, judging by Richards's notes, the defense attorneys continued their inexplicable silence until the end.

In his closing arguments, Charles Evans presented broad observations. Richards's notations written in brief phrases capture the essence of Evans's attempts at persuasion. The first passages suggested the prosecution failed to prove its case. Evans's remarks included these key elements:

The [illegible] court [illegible] presumption shall not convict without probable presumptive proof that the Child was born alive. The concealment [illegible] unless the circumstances be [put?] as think satisfy the jury that the Mother destroyed her infant. It must appear[:] That their [there] was a concealment of the Birth. That the presumption is so strong as to make the Jury to believe that the mother murdered the Child. It must be proved that the Child was born alive. It must be proved that the mother murdered it. The jury must be convinced that the Person [Susanna Cox] was the Mother of the Child.

After repeating several times the jury must be convinced the child was born alive, Evans reminded the twelve men yet again they should believe that the Child was born alive.

And they [illegible]murdered the child. That is that she killed it [maliciously?] and knowingly. Otherwise she must be acquitted. It is not necessary that Witnesses should be produced who saw the Child alive & the Mother kill it. But just presumptive evidence should be produced as not to have a doubt on the minds of the jury, for if they doubt they must acquit.

The statement, "It is not necessary that witnesses should be produced who saw the child alive and the mother kill it," *is* damning. Although Evans undoubtedly meant the prosecution's evidence was "presumptive," he left the impression the prosecution was relieved from the duty of providing a witness to murder. Furthermore, Franks did not even need to furnish a witness to a live birth. The jury could simply imagine the baby was born alive and Susanna murdered it. That simple decree left the door open for the jury to rely on their meager medical knowledge and opinions, and it rendered the testimony of the doctors superfluous and of little consequence.

To his credit, Evans repeated several times that the jury should be convinced the baby was born alive. He might have hoped that the jury recalled the testimonies of the two doctors who cast shadows of doubt about a live birth, but he did not drive home Baum's statement that "children born in this way are generally born dead." Incredibly, the jurors ignored that possibility. Evans then said:

> There [is] no positive proof of any thing except that she was the mother of the child & that appears entirely by her Confession which by my under[standing] of the Law and Justice ought to be taken altogether.

By "Confession," Evans was not alluding to a confession of guilt, but Susanna's confession the child was hers. Evans's next argument contained the statement, "The broken jaw, the tow, and the appearance of the child are [illegible] however no proof of her guilt." Rather than exonerating Susanna, this declaration may actually have cemented the condition of the infant's body in the minds of the jury.

> The Broken jaw, the tow, & the appearance of the Child are [illegible] however no proof of her guilt. The Broken jaw may well be accounted for by the situation of Child in the Closet. The Tow was [illegible] not bound to account for but it is in evidence that the House was open & any person had access to it. Is there any proof that the Tow was put in before the death of the Child for even if she put it in after the death, she cannot be convicted.

From this point on, Evans turned to generalities concerning Susanna's character.

A strong evidence of Guilt is flight. The Prisoner remained. An evidence of Guilt is prevarication & contradiction on the part of the Prisoner. The Person has been consistent, [illegible] & prompt in her account.

The person naturally humane and virtuous [illegible] a [turn?] to crime. Which shook humanity. Yet her character has always been good.

In their closing arguments, the defense team failed to challenge the lack of clarity with which Otto answered questions. They ignored Baum's statement about stillbirth. They failed to stress other possible scenarios that might account for the baby's death. The defense could have pointed out that if the baby was born choking on blood and dying, it would have been natural for Susanna to staunch the flow of blood with the bit of tow. She may have tried to absorb the blood with the tow so the baby could breathe, thus trying to *save* her baby, not *kill* it.

According to Susanna's confession, she gave birth around 4:30 in the morning on February 14. One can surmise she was terrified, confused, and in pain—and she was certainly alone. The defense team did not mention the exhaustion Susanna faced after giving birth. Her physical and emotional state may have clouded her judgment, even if she experienced no difficulties during labor.

Fear of losing her position with the Geehrs was the underlying reason for Susanna's concealing her pregnancy, and she allegedly went to great lengths to hide the little body. She probably did not want her dead infant to spend eternity in a hole in the washhouse. But having given birth on a cold February morning, her options were limited for disposal of the body. The ground in the Schneider family cemetery near the farmhouse was probably frozen, preventing her from digging a grave. Furthermore, the cemetery is situated at the top of a gentle slope near the farmhouse. Although the cemetery is enclosed within a stone wall, Susanna would have had to trudge up the incline to the cemetery across bare ground and patches of ice and snow. Had she made this sad journey, she would have been clearly visible from the farmhouse. In addition, at a future point in time, someone might have discovered a newly dug grave, so the Schneider family cemetery was probably not a good place to hide a body. Also, the stream in front of the washhouse was likely frozen, so she was unable to cast the body in its waters. Clearly, she did not opt to leave the body exposed to the elements or predators. But it is also true she probably had no long-term plan as to what to do with the body. Over the short term, it seemed humane to wrap the small body in a coat and place it in the wash-house. From this viewpoint, one can speculate Susanna was not "hiding" the body, but providing her little son a makeshift grave.

Until the closing arguments, open access to the washhouse was left unexplored by her defense. If the baby was born alive, as the jury seemed to believe, it was not necessarily Susanna who killed it. Anyone could have killed the infant and disposed of the body. Susanna could have been taking the blame for the father—her mental acumen would have provided for a malleable personality.

Nagle admitted in court that Susanna divulged the father's name to him, but he was never pressed to reveal the identity. Certainly the father should have been regarded as a suspect, as he had a motive to murder the infant. If the child had been born alive, the father, not wanting to be implicated, could have murdered it. Furthermore, in the interim between birth and discovery, many other people entered the washhouse. Jacob Geehr said in his testimony that members of his own family frequented the building, yet no other possible suspects were ever considered.

Failure to identify the father was not the only error made by the defense. Little thought was given to alternative explanations concerning the infant's death and the condition of the corpse. The infant's jaw may have been dislocated in any number of ways. The body had been removed from and replaced in the hole multiple times. Perhaps the jaw was frozen to the coat in which the baby had been wrapped or to the tow or even on a bit of stone or the wall. If the tow were frozen to the jaw, the jaw could have separated in attempts to remove it. Geehr, confessing to no knowledge that the bundle was a baby, certainly would not have handled the body with care when he first removed it from the hole. Furthermore, if Susanna tried to clear the mouth and throat of blood, she could have unwittingly applied too much pressure. Numerous reasons account for a dislocated jaw, but none were explored by the court.

Importantly, the court neglected to discuss the one event that could account for the condition of the body. The birthing process is violent in and of itself. A newborn, arriving facedown, does not arrive in a nice, neat package. It is covered with vernix, placental fluid, and other matter that make the baby a slippery, messy bundle. Because Susanna delivered alone, she not only had to suffer the pain of labor, but play doctor as well. From a squatting position, the infant could have erupted, face down, and hit the floor solidly, dislocating its jaw before Susanna was able to catch it. The bleeding jaw would have caused the infant to strangle on its own blood, so Susanna might have attempted to absorb the blood with tow. As the aftershock of childbirth hit Susanna, her attempts to rescue the baby may have been too late or too clumsy—or carried out in a state of panic.

Susanna was alone during the birth, and this certainly could have been a contributing factor in causing the infant's death. In 1809, America was a developing nation. A recent study of developing nations found nineteen percent of infant mortalities, in areas such as Ghana for instance, are caused by injuries sustained during birth. The study found this number could be significantly reduced simply with the presence of an assistant.

A number of scenarios at the time of birth are possible. Perhaps the baby had not even been born when things began to go terribly wrong. Its head may have been large and slow to move through the birth canal. With no one to help, Susanna would have to pull the baby out herself, injuring it in the process. Maybe, as Baum seemed to indicate, the cord was around the newborn's neck.

After the baby was born, Susanna would still have to deliver the placenta. During the entire lengthy and exhausting process, her body would have been trembling from her exertions. She would have been hard put to care for herself, let alone an injured newborn. The baby might have died by the time she started to recover and turn her attention toward him. Therefore, she would have believed it was stillborn.

Part of Jacob Geehr's testimony supports the possibility that problems during the birth of the Cox infant led to its tragic end. Susanna was strong. A laborer her entire life, she was in her prime at twenty-four. Yet Geehr's testimony clearly stated Susanna was not at work on February 14. Something affected her so badly that she was unable to perform her duties. Geehr further stated that, although Susanna was "up" on the fifteenth, it wasn't until the sixteenth and seventeenth that she was "about the House."

A difficult birth also supports Otto's findings. There was no blood in the ears or eyes that would result from head trauma after a deliberate blow. If Susanna had, in fact, delivered a fatal blow to the newborn, there would have been evidence of bruising and abrasions, in addition to the dislocated jaw.

The defense also failed to use the relatively new penal system to their advantage. As indicated, beginning in 1794, Pennsylvania imposed the death penalty only in cases involving first-degree murder and treason. But, first-degree murder meant the crime must be proven to have been willful, deliberate, and premeditated. A premeditated murder is characterized by purpose, previous consideration, and some degree of planning. In the absence of proven premeditation, all other murders were treated as second degree and punishable by prison time. Based on the evidence presented, premeditation does not neatly describe events that unfolded on that fateful day.

The defense team's greatest failure involves the issue of reasonable doubt. They should have reminded the jury that they must be convinced beyond doubt of Susanna's guilt. Yet the defense missed obvious opportunities to emphasize Otto's uncertainties and Baum's testimony that "Children born in this way are generally dead."

In his article, "Susanna Cox: Her Crime and its Expiation," Louis Richards correctly pointed out that "no testimony was adduced on the part of the defense." They cast aside opportunities to cross-examine witnesses or ask obvious questions, they provided no alternative explanations, they neglected to pressure Nagle for the identity of the father, they disregarded ambiguous and contradictory testimony, they gave no thought to summarizing the preceding into a case for reasonable doubt, they did not ask the court for leniency, and they failed to qualify the murder as second degree—they simply failed on all counts. And their many failures cost Susanna Cox her life.

The jury quickly returned a guilty verdict. At this point, President Judge John Spayd could have stepped in and overturned the verdict. Precedence, important in 1809 law, would have allowed Spayd to say the prosecution did not meet the burden of proof. In 1759, seventeen-year-old Margaretta Kirchin of Lancaster, Pennsylvania, was convicted of murdering her illegitimate infant. The judge at the trial reported to the governor that her guilt was unclear and she was pardoned, despite the fact that a jury found her guilty. Certainly, Spayd had the governor's ear. Trial judges' viewpoints and recommendations were foremost in determining who received clemency from the governor. It appears, however, Spayd neither thought enough nor cared enough to intercede on Susanna's behalf.

Various accounts report Susanna was returned to court for sentencing on April 8, the day following the rendering of the verdict. To the contrary, the court docket indicates Susanna was tried and sentenced on April 7, all in the space of four hours and fifty minutes. Although some accounts state the jury deliberated between three and four hours, records show the *entire* trial lasted four hours and fifty minutes.

When the trial ended, popular versions hold that it was in a halting, grief-stricken voice that Spayd conveyed the verdict and sentence to Susanna and the citizens of Reading:

"The sentence of the court is that Susanna Cox be hanged by the neck until she be dead."

Her sentence was probably translated for her. She bowed her head and wept.

10

SLINKING OFF ANONYMOUSLY

Her neighbor, well remember we—
Merz was his second name—
He recklessly led her astray
By lust's unhallowed flame.

—"A NEW DIRGE CONTAINING THE HISTORY OF SUSANNA COX"

Why does the father of the Cox baby matter? Knowing the father's name two hundred years after the event will not change the course of history. In that respect, his name does not matter *now*, but it did matter in 1809. At the time, men were often tried for "bastardy and fornication." Bringing fathers to court for their illegitimate children was the only way the mothers of these children could seek recompense for the cost of raising a child alone. Obviously, this would be better for the community, because the community could avoid dipping into its coffers to care for unwed mothers and their offspring. Fathers of children born out of wedlock, if found guilty of paternity, were compelled to pay expenses for a certain number of years. Berks County court records from 1808 and 1809 indicate that seven years of support was average. In that amount of time it was presumed the mother would have married or remarried. The Reading court records from the time are peppered with bastardy and fornication cases, but as expected, the name of Susanna Cox is not among them.

Several possibilities regarding paternity of the Cox baby present themselves. The first hint at his name was allegedly given by Susanna herself after the trial. In her confession, written by an anonymous third party and dated June 8, 1809, she allegedly stated the father's initials were "P.M." Rightly or wrongly, this name gradually morphed into "Peter Mertz."

Pennsylvania Germans tended to use the same first names repeatedly in single-family units and in extended families. This practice causes major headaches for researchers when they attempt to sort out specific individuals. If the father was truly Peter Mertz, a possible candidate for a man by that name was the youngest son of immigrant Johannes Märtz (Mertz, Merz) from Stockhausen in Württemberg. Peter Mertz was born in Oley Township in 1769 and died in Orwigsburg, Schuylkill County, in 1833. The Johannes Märtz family, however, is more closely associated with Longswamp Township in Berks County and the Kutztown area of Maxatawny Township. In 1793, Peter Mertz married Catharine Phillips of Bern Township. Nagle testified the father of the Cox infant was a married man.

In *The Passing Scene*, Volume 15, George and Gloria Jean Meiser indicate that "according to trial records—a Mr. Mertz lived with his wife and two children" at the Wegman-Houp farm down the road from the Schneider-Geehr farm. The Meisers maintain Mertz was a "tenant farmer," which seems plausible. They also note they never saw the missing trial notes, so they may have used Richards's transcripts, which say only that the father of the Cox infant was a married man. Attempts to confirm the Meisers' additional information from original sources proved unsuccessful, but the ballad of Susanna Cox uses the surname Mertz and identifies the man as a neighbor.

Richards mentioned trial notes taken by Marks John Biddle. Biddle's account, however, was probably brief, lacking the detail seen in Richards's transcripts. If Biddle gave additional details about the father, Richards would have stated so. Yet Richards himself dismissed Biddle's account, saying, "According to the notes of trial taken by Mr. Biddle, the facts developed were as already been stated."

The current owners of the Schneider–Geehr farm, the Hetricks, the third generation of the family now living there, never heard of anyone by the name Mertz. There are no court records in Berks County between 1808 and 1810 showing a Peter Mertz, or a man with the initials P.M., in Berks County fathering an illegitimate child. Because bastardy and fornication charges were attempts by the courts to induce fathers to care for their illegitimate children, the absence of Mertz's name in the court dockets is explained by the fact that no child survived. Although the initials "P—M—" appear in Susanna's printed confession, and the surname Mertz appears in Cox-related articles and on broadsides published throughout the nineteenth and twentieth centuries, this is not conclusive evidence of Mertz's paternity.

Today, Jacob Geehr is often targeted in oral tradition as the father of the baby and the villain who left Susanna to suffer the consequences. Geehr certainly had easy access to her. Also, because Esther Geehr was sickly, Geehr may have had ample motive for seducing Susanna. Geehr was also part of Susanna's life four years prior, when she apparently gave birth to a stillborn child. Naturally, separate pregnancies may have resulted from different fathers, but Geehr had motive and opportunity. Also, because Geehr was Susanna's employer, he had clout.

Still other possibilities for paternity exist. The name Daniel Schneider was common in southeastern Pennsylvania. Some Daniel Schneiders were closely related to the Schneiders at the family farm on Monocacy Creek. Even if they were not residing at the Schneider–Geehr farm at the time Susanna lived there, locals named Daniel Schneider were in the area. In the Berks County court records, one entry stands out—a January 5, 1808, bastardy and fornication case that involved Daniel Schneider. Mary Bopp won a case against him for support of her illegitimate child. Schneider was to pay $14 for her "lying in" expenses. Furthermore, he was to pay a weekly sum of $1 until the child reached the age of seven, a $55 fee upon birth, and a fine to the Commonwealth. These were not inconsequential costs.

Beyond illegitimacy, there is another link between Susanna's case and that of Daniel Schneider. Frederick Smith was the attor-

ney defending Schneider against the charges of bastardy and fornication. The court ruled against Schneider. Therefore, as expensive
as his child with Mary Bopp was, Schneider knew the penalty for
his behavior. If he fathered Susanna's child, he had motive for
removing both Susanna and the baby. And if Susanna was pregnant by Schneider previously, she was perhaps proving to be too
much of a temptation and threat. In short, if Susanna had a history
of unwanted pregnancies, Schneider had a history of unwanted
children.

If rape is discounted, the father likely would have needed time
to coerce Susanna into an affair. Schneider's and Geehr's presence
on the Schneider–Geehr farm would have gone unnoticed, and
both men would have had time to form a relationship with
Susanna. Frequent visits by Peter Mertz, on the other hand, might
have been suspect. In any event, the father of the Cox baby was
probably someone Susanna knew and trusted.

Other possibilities exist as to the father's identity. The infant
was born in February, so he would have been conceived the previous spring when plowing and planting required extra helpers at the
farm. Any number of men would have been present at this time
and could have been the father.

Ultimately, the defense should have pursued the identity of the
father more aggressively. It seems odd they did not, for they should
have recalled a case from the 1780s. A young woman named Elizabeth Wilson (ca. 1762–86) gave birth to twins but was wrongfully
hanged for their deaths. The father remained anonymous until
additional information came to light. Wilson was a farm girl from
Chester County, who was seduced by promises of marriage by
Joseph Deshong. Little is known of Deshong, who is called Smith
in some sources. What is known is that Deshong had no intention
of honoring his promises and Wilson returned to her family pregnant with twins. Deshong followed her home, perhaps afraid she
would name him as the father. He lured Wilson, with the newly
born twins, from the home. He savagely murdered the babies and
again disappeared. Hunters found the twins, crushed, in the nearby
woods. Wilson was charged with their murder. Reportedly, she was
so traumatized by the death of her babes that she never spoke

another word after their murder. In Wilson's case, she had the sympathy of the Supreme Council, who pardoned her. Her brother William, or by some accounts Amos, raced back from Philadelphia on the day of the hanging with the pardon in hand. Legend has it that the Schuylkill River was flooded, but somehow William crossed the swollen river. The delay, however, cost his sister her life. He arrived, tragically, only minutes too late. In agony, he no longer wanted to live among the human race and became known as the Pennsylvania Hermit. Of interest, the person who penned Wilson's reprieve was a relative of Marks John Biddle, Charles Biddle, Vice President of the Supreme Council of the Commonwealth.

The father in the Cox case had motivation to destroy the infant. Married men and their families suffered extreme humiliation should their cases come to court. Not only were charges of bastardy and fornication embarrassing, as noted in the case of Daniel Schneider, they were expensive. Court fees, attorney costs, and child support caused fathers to abandon their families and seek anonymity in distant places. In some cases, such as that of Susanna Cox, they remained silent concerning their culpability.

Consequently, women bore the burden of rearing the child alone in a society where she and the child became outcasts and faced financial hardship. Unwed mothers who murdered their infants out of fear often suffered the consequences, while fathers slinked off anonymously, escaping their responsibility. A few cases were ignored by the courts for fear of implicating and embarrassing a respected citizen.

In fairness to them, evidence against Peter Mertz, Jacob Geehr, or Daniel Schneider is circumstantial at best. It no longer matters who fathered the child, except for one key element. If the father had shouldered responsibility, Susanna may have felt less trapped. If she, in fact, murdered her tiny son, she might not have resorted to such an extreme measure if she anticipated forthcoming support from the father.

For her crime, real or not, Susanna paid the ultimate price. The courts let her down. By any measure, Justice of the Peace Peter Nagle, the defense team of Marks John Biddle, Charles Evans, and Frederick Smith, President Judge John Spayd, and the jurors cared little or not at all about questioning the father. Ironically, from a historical perspective, these men set themselves at risk of being judged themselves—perhaps even more harshly than the father. Potentially, their haste and dismissal of Susanna Cox will forever tarnish their otherwise stellar reputations, for history has a way of perpetually judging events. Had they known that future generations would savor a keen interest in the case, they might have performed differently.

Above: The Schneider–Geehr farm as it exists today.

The washhouse as it appeared about 1900.
SCHWENKFELDER LIBRARY & HERITAGE CENTER

Creek-side view of the lower level of the washhouse. Today, the top structure is entirely gone and the doorway shows what early reporters referred to as "the cave."

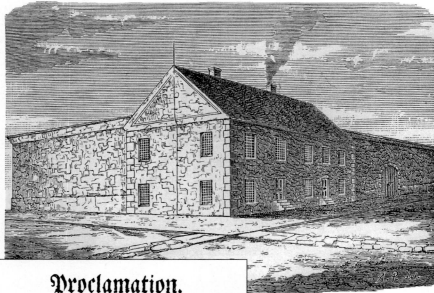

Proclamation.

Es wird hiermit allen Friedensrichtern, dem Coroner, den Constabels und allen andern bürgerlichen Beamten, in der County Berks, Nachricht gegeben, daß sie, und jeder von ihnen, sich in der Stadt Reading, in ersagter County, auf den Samstag den z e h n t e n Tag des nächsten Juny, um 9 Uhr Vormittags, ersagten Tages, einzufinden haben, um alsdann und daselbst dem Scheriff der ersagten County Beystand zu leisten, um Friede und gute Ordnung zu erhalten bey der Hinrichtung einer gewißen S u s a n n a C o x, welche jezt in dem gemeinen Gefängnis der ersagten County gefangen sizt und, auf den ersagten Tag, auf dem gewöhnlichen Platz der Hinrichtung, hingerichtet werden soll.

Gegeben unter meiner Hand den 19ten Tag des May, im Jahr unsers Herrn ein tausend acht hundert und neun und im drey und dreyßigsten Jahre der Unabhängigkeit von America.

G e o r g e M a r x, Scheriff.
G o t t e r h a l t e d i e R e p u b l i k.

Above: The Reading jail as it appeared around 1809, from Morton L. Montgomery's History of Reading, Pennsylvania.

Above: Proclamation that Susanna Cox was to be hanged on June 10, 1809, as printed in Der Readinger Adler. READEX, HUGH M. MORRIS LIBRARY, UNIVERSITY OF DELAWARE

The Berks County courthouse as it appeared around 1809, from Morton L. Montgomery's History of Reading, Pennsylvania.

Susanna Cox on her way to the gallows as portrayed in a ca. 1890 romanticized newspaper account. The caption reads, "Lutz's men cleared the way for Susanna's royal progress up to Mount Penn"—a far cry from a lonely girl following her coffin to her doom. ROUGHWOOD COLLECTION

Philip Reinhold Pauli (1742–1815), the German Reformed minister who tended Susanna Cox in her last days. FIRST UNITED CHURCH OF CHRIST, READING, PENNSYLVANIA

An early woodcut showing a horse-drawn cart being led from under a gallows. This image illustrates the type of gallows used in Susanna Cox's hanging.

Reime

über die Bekehrung der Susanna ?
vor ihrer Hinrichtung am 10ten Juny, 1809, in Berks Caunty, we-
gen der Ermordung ihres unehelichen Kindes.

Eilend's kömmt heran die Stunde,
Da man mir das Leben nimmt.
Wie ich hör' aus Scheriff's Munde,
So ist mir der Tag bestimmt:
Junius, der zehnte Tag,
Nimmt man mir das Leben ab.

2.

Vater! Laß mich Gnade finden;
Gieb mir doch nur Trost in Sinn,
Die ich, wegen großen Sünden,
So betrübt und traurig bin;
Sprich', mein Gott, noch eh' ich ruh',
Meiner Seele Gnade zu.

3.

Großer Gott, voll Lieb' und Treue,
Laß doch meiner Seelen noch
Ihre späte Buß und Reue
Vor dir etwas gelten noch;
Denk', o Gott! nicht mehr daran
Was ich Sünder hab' gethan.

4.

Sprich', o Gott, zu meiner Seelen:
"Heut hast du noch Gnad' erlangt;"
Daß mich keine Schmerzen quälen
In der letzten Todes Angst.
Regale mir auch durch Christi Blut,
Mach's mir an meinem Ende gut.

5.

Meine Seele ist betrübet,
Durch die große Missethat;
Weil ich Mord hab ausgeübet
Nicht an Gott geglaubet hab';
Das sechst' Gebot hab ich verübt
Das siebente auch noch betrübt.

6.

Laß, Herr Jesu, die Gebote
Mir im Tod nicht schädlich seyn;
Vergieb sie mir noch vor dem Tode
Und laß mich selig schlafen ein.
Sprich nur zu mir, wie du am Creuz
Zum Schächer sprachst, bin ich erfreut.

7.

Du, Herr Jesu, wollst mir Sünder
Heute noch gnädig seyn;

Und die Zahlen meiner Stunden
Wiederum doch nehmen ein;
So will ich von Herzen dich
Preisen dafür ewiglich.

8.

Keine Buße geht verlohren,
Sprachst du dort zum Zacheo,
Heut ist Heil dir wiederfahren,
Deinem Hause geht es wohl.
Herr Jesu kehr auch bey mir ein;
Sprich auch, ich will dir gnädig seyn.

9.

Heut, sprichst du am Creuz zum Schächer,
Sollst du bey mir im Paradies
Noch bey mir seyn, bey Gott zur Rechten,
Gieb nur getrost dein Leben hin,
Sprich auch zu mir an meinem End:
Komm auch in mein Jerusalem.

Innerliches Seelen-Gespräch.

Seele.

Bald muß ich mein Leben enden,
O Seel', wo geht die Reise hin,
Wie du gesäet, so mußt du erndten;
Doch hoff ich, Gott ist gnädig mir.
Gleich wie man hier gesäet hat,
So erndtet man auch dort die Saat.

Jesus.

Seele, gieb dich nur zufrieden;
Dein Weinen ist vor Gott erhört,
Ich hab die Thränen aufgeschrieben;
Sey nur getrost, du bist erlöst,
Stell all' dein Trauren ein und preiß'
Die Gnad auf deiner Himmels-Reiß.

Seele.

Also kann ich nichts verliehren;
Leget man mich gleich in's Grab;
Jesus will mich herrlich zieren,
Weil ich ihn im Glauben hab'.
Ich sterbe gern, wie's Gott gefällt
Und scheide fröhlich von der Welt.

Trost Reime.

Komm' Seele, komm', ile und säume dich nicht,
Laß fahren dein Weinen und Sterben-Gedicht,
Dir sind schon geöffnet de Himmels-Rings-Mauren,
Wo ewiglich Freude, wo ewig kein Trauren
Laß fahren hienieden den leiblichen Leben,
Dort hab' ich der Seele die Gnade gegeben.
Im Himmel, im Himmel sind Freuden so viel,
Da sind die Begnadigte und singen ihr Spiel;
Sie singen, sie loben, sie preisen stets Gott,
Der alle Bekehrten mit Gnade begabt.
Herr Jesu, ach schenk' ein Sünder auf's Neu',
Daß er mit den Engeln mög stimmen hinein,
Wo Freude die Fülle, wo Herrlichkeit wohnt,
Wo alle Begnadigten werden belohnt.

Gedruckt auf Begehren des Verfassers....Gedruckt bey J. Ritter und Comp....Preiß 6 Cents.

The "Reime" broadside, printed by John Ritter between May 16 and June 10, 1809. HISTORICAL SOCIETY OF BERKS COUNTY.

A NEW MOURNFUL SONG,

CONTAINING THE HISTORY OF

SUSANNA COX

Who was Hanged in Reading for Infanticide, in the Year 1809.

FROM THE GERMAN.

Take notice now ye people all,
  And hear what will be said
About a very gloomy case,
  Of a deluded maid.

She served as maid, in Oley long,
  With one named Jacob Gehr,
Her name was MISS SUSANNA COX,
  I heard it mentioned there.

No education she received,
  She knew but what she saw;
The will of God she did not know,
  Nor aught about his law.

To most people it is known
  How in the world it goes;—
They who the Scriptures do not know
  Will do just what they chose.

Her neighbor who is known to us,
  Whose name was Mertz, withal,
Seduced her with his fleshly lust
  And brought her to her fall.

'Twas similar in Adam's time
  The Bible teaches us,
When the Old Serpent, loving crime,
  Did Mother Eve seduce.

Through her seduction entered death
  The world when it began;
So went it with Susanna Cox,
  By this deceptive man.

The law he held in disrespect,
  And scorned to keep his hand
From what the Scriptures do forbid
  In that heptade command.

As married man he her seduced
  And brought her in distress ;
He may repent, if not refused,
  At some time after death.

She had this matter not revealed
  So much ashamed was she:
She thought no person would take note
  Of her delivery.

In eighteen hundred and ninth year,
  In February, fourteenth day,
At early morn, at half past four,
  Her child was born, they say.

As this poor sinner, viciously
  Deceived had been, you see,
She did her newborn child remove
  To long eternity.

As soon as the discoverers saw
  The murder had been dealt,
She was arrested by the law,
  And asked to own her guilt.

A jury soon was summoned, then,
  Who did investigate
This helpless sinner's case, and name
  Her sentence or her fate.

She plead before the jurors there,
  For mercy she did pray,
But still they found her guilty sore
  Of murder, first degree.

They led her int' the Courthouse then,
  Before Judge SPAYD—quite near,
Where she her dreadful sentence–death
  With weeping had to hear.

You may imagine for yourself,
  How sorrowful she felt
To wait her execution—death—
  Her blood was to be spilt.

The death-warrant was written soon
  For this poor maid alone,
And taken to the governor
  Out in Lancaster town.

A man who was compassionate
  She hast'ly sent before,
Unto the govenor of state,
  Who plead and sued for her.

But he for her no pardon found:
  Alas! She must be hung
Already on the tenth of June,
  To show the world 'twas wrong.

The death-warrant was soon returned,
  And then to her was read:—
To God she prayed most fervently
  For grace till she was dead.

She was in her repentance by
  The clergy taught redress,
For she repented candidly,
  And did her sins confess.

From prison she was taken out,
  About eleven o'clock,
Upon the execution–place—
  It caused a moral shock.

She cautioned all mankind around,
  The young especially,
And said, "Take an example now,
  By my ill fate to-day.

She knelt upon the earth in prayer,
  And asked the Lord alone,
That he would all her sins forgive,
  Which ever she had done.

Her weeping was so sorrowful,
  As on her knees she lay;
Her tear-drops fell upon the earth—
  They wept for her that day,

She said, "I go t'eternity
  Now instantly. O God,
Take me into thy kingdom, see,
  Reject me sinner not!"

She's executed afterward:—
  A lamentable deed!
And after seventeen minutes time,
  Her parting soul had fled.

And after she was dead, in vain,
  The doctors tried their skill
To bring her back to life again,
  But all too late and ill.

And he who did this song compose
  And earnestly did dictate,
Did all this misery behold,
  Was near the judgment seat.

Ye people all on earth give ear,
  Take this example here,
When people are so ignorant,
  How they at last may fare.

She did not live in pleasure long
  Ere she was in the snare,
She brought her whole life's journey on
  To four and twenty years.

A typical ballad of Susanna Cox broadside, printed in English by an anonymous printer. Note that the sheet has "from the German" printed on it. RUSSELL AND CORINNE EARNEST COLLECTION

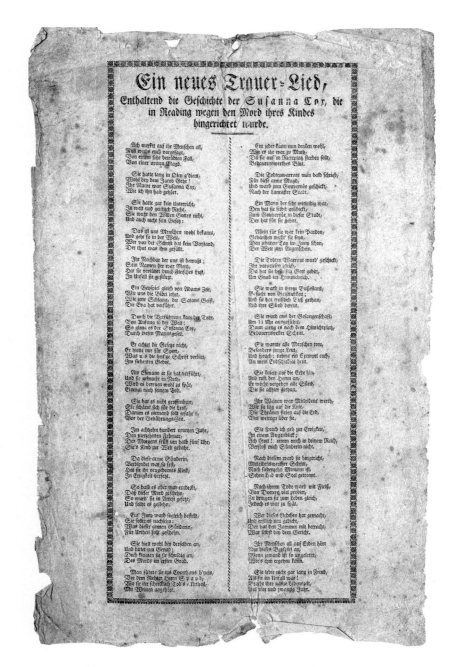

A typical Susanna Cox broadside ballad, probably printed in Allentown, Pennsylvania, by Henrich Ebner, ca. 1825.

RUSSELL AND CORINNE EARNEST COLLECTION

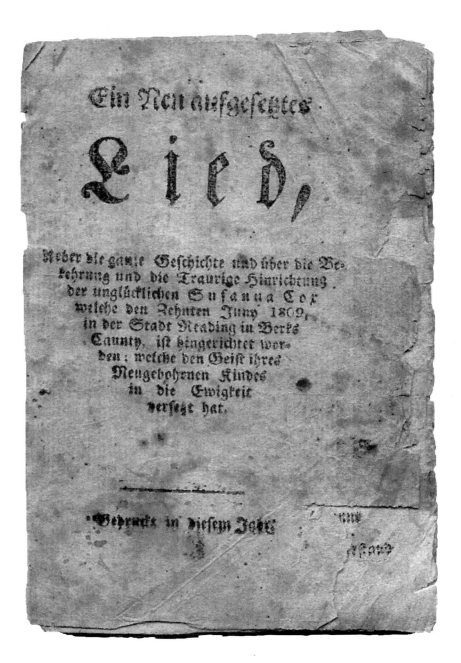

The only surviving example of an early printing of the ballad of Susanna Cox, 1809. The imprint says, "printed in this year." The hundreds of German-language broadsides that followed copied this text with minor changes. FRANKLIN AND MARSHALL COLLEGE, LANCASTER, PENNSYLVANIA

Louis Richards (1842–1924), the Berks County historian who transcribed the now-missing Cox case court records. HISTORICAL SOCIETY OF BERKS COUNTY

The effigy of Susanna Cox ascending the thirteen steps to be "launched into eternity" at the Kutztown Folk Festival, circa 1965. ROUGHWOOD COLLECTION

Visitors at the Kutztown Folk Festival in July 2009 watch the effigy of Susanna Cox hang from the gallows after hearing June DeTurk tell the story. KYLE WEAVER

11

A LAST HOPE

Then to the Governor was sent,
Who lived in Lancaster,
The warrant which contained her doom,
For his own signature.

—"A NEW DIRGE CONTAINING THE HISTORY OF SUSANNA COX"

A ppeals were not standard procedure in the Early Republic. Some cases were brought before the governor, but a family member or another interested party was needed to intercede on the prisoner's behalf. After the guilty verdict was delivered to Susanna Cox, her defense team apparently dropped the case. An unknown person, however, petitioned the governor in Lancaster, which at that time was the capital of Pennsylvania. This person perhaps thought that even if the governor was unable to legally overturn the verdict, he would at least have the power to mete out a different form of punishment—one without bloodshed. Some accounts claim Barbara Katzenmoyer, Susanna's sister, rallied the city and sent a petition to the governor. More than likely, the appeal for clemency consisted of a simple letter written by an individual. Broadsides containing the Susanna Cox ballad support this possibility. The anonymous petitioner remains a matter of conjecture. Any member of the Cox family might have petitioned the governor. Rev. Philip Reinhold Pauli or Dr. John Christian Baum,

both of whom visited Susanna in jail, may have presented a petition. The defense attorneys cannot be completely ruled out, nor
any members of the jury. Rumors persisted, depending on the
source, that from one to three jurors held out against the guilty verdict, although certainly not for long. But some jurors might have
regretted their vote and attempted to right their wrong. The author
of the original ballad of Susanna Cox is another possibility. The
ballad presents a sympathetic view of Susanna, and the author
wrote in the ballad that he was present at her trial. Whoever petitioned the governor would have done so in the days and weeks following April 7.

Governor Simon Snyder became Susanna's last hope. The
ambitious Snyder was new to his office, having been inaugurated in
December 1808. A handsome man with dark hair and aristocratic
features, Snyder had humble beginnings as a tanning and currying
apprentice. The trade, however, did not interest him. In his twen-
ties, he opened a store and ran a gristmill, both located in Selinsgrove. He then became involved in politics, serving in the
Pennsylvania House of Representatives from 1797 to 1807. Snyder
first ran for the office of governor under the Democratic-Republican
party as an advocate for the poor in 1805, challenging the incumbent, Thomas McKean. McKean was a Revolutionary War hero
who had the support of influential men of the time, such as Peter
Muhlenberg, son of Lutheran church patriarch Henry Melchior
Muhlenberg, and war hero Joseph Hiester. Like Snyder, Muhlenberg and Hiester were of Pennsylvania German descent, but hostil-
ity towards Snyder by Muhlenberg thwarted Snyder's early political
ambitions. Editorials in an Easton-area newspaper, *The American
Eagle*, showed Muhlenberg's influence was enough to keep Snyder
from being elected in 1805.

The 1805 loss of an election did not deter Snyder, who ran again
in 1808. It is commonly reported in accounts about Susanna Cox
that Snyder again ran against the incumbent Thomas McKean. This
is untrue, for McKean was impeached in 1807. He was able to fin-
ish his term, but only through the efforts of his powerful friends
was he saved from a lengthy trial. This time around, Snyder ran
against Federalist James Ross and none other than Judge John

Spayd. It was at the urging of Frederick Smith, Susanna's defense attorney, that Spayd entered the election. Smith held Spayd in high regard, feeling he would have a significant advantage over Ross and Snyder. Spayd ran as a Quid, a little-remembered third party. He had the backing of Christian Jacob Hütter, who published two influential newspapers in Easton, the *Pennsylvania Herald and Easton Intelligencer* and the *Northampton Correspondent*.

The newspapers of southeastern Pennsylvania engaged in a nasty debate over the three candidates. It was a bitter battle that found Snyder victorious. Spayd placed second only in areas where he resided, Northampton and Berks counties. Otherwise, Snyder and Ross vied for the lead. Spayd suffered a dismal loss, considering his many influential supporters, especially the Muhlenberg and Hiester families to whom he was related by marriage. While no direct evidence suggests Snyder's and Spayd's electoral animosity had any bearing on the Cox case, one has to wonder if their historic competition introduced bias in the response to the anonymous petitioner's plea for clemency.

In "Susanna Cox: Her Crime and its Expiation," Richards cited possible reasons for Snyder's decision to continue with the execution. Although the governor felt the signing of death warrants to be his most painful duty, he signed Susanna's warrant perhaps to avoid second-guessing the court's decision. According to Richards, nineteenth-century courts were largely expected to stand alone. In an era of newly developed statehood, little likelihood existed that a jury's verdict would be subject to interference, and the appeals system was scarcely known. In some ways, judges had more power at their disposal than other governing bodies.

Perhaps Snyder espoused the view that *someone* had to serve as an example to unwed mothers who might consider killing unwanted infants. History may never know Snyder's thinking with regard to signing Susanna Cox's death warrant; however, in 1809, and again in 1811, Snyder asked the Pennsylvania State Legislature to abolish the death penalty. Although Snyder's proposals fell on deaf ears, the Cox case may have served as a catalyst for his attempts.

12

SEDUCED BY THE DEVIL

But she no pardon could obtain,
For she was to be hung
As early as the tenth of June,
To warn both old and young.

—"A NEW DIRGE CONTAINING THE HISTORY OF SUSANNA COX"

Throughout the Early Republic, laws were improving, offering greater protection to vulnerable members of society, such as the poor and uneducated. The rate of executions was slowing, the establishment of penitentiaries growing.

Lawyers became more sophisticated, as did the laws themselves. Legal procedures were standardized across the country. Acts such as swearing were deemed unworthy of harsh punishment. The introduction of professional standards for investigating crimes became the norm. The medical profession advanced its technologies and procedures. Autopsies became routine in questionable deaths. Bloodletting tools were relegated to museums where they belonged.

In addition, Americans examined motives and reasons behind crimes and came to recognize and remedy inequalities in the judicial system. Early Americans threw off the yoke of the inflexible system they inherited and embraced their new world, the one they created for themselves. Enlightenment came, but it came too late for Susanna Cox.

Susanna was not only a victim of her time, she was also the victim of bad timing. Similar cases leading up to 1809 remained in the recent memories of citizens of southeast Pennsylvania. In 1758, Elizabeth Graul was convicted of murdering her illegitimate child in Berks County. Nine years later, in 1767, Catherine Krebs was convicted on the same charge. Both women were hanged in Reading. Sarah Keating was charged in 1804 with the murder of her illegitimate child, but she was acquitted. Richards stated that between 1790 and 1809, five women in other Pennsylvania counties were charged with the murder of illegitimate children. From a historical standpoint regarding Berks County in general and Reading in particular, no unwed mother convicted of the murder of her infant had provided a moral example to the women of that county in more than forty years.

As public sentiment moved away from capital punishment, certain cases caused even the most soft-hearted to harden their viewpoint. One of these that likely had bearing on the Cox case was that of sixteen-year-old Mary Meloy of nearby Lancaster, who was arrested on similar charges. A newspaper account citing the Meloy case was published concurrently when Governor Snyder was pondering Susanna's death warrant.

Meloy apparently murdered her infant son on May 3, 1809. According to a Maryland newspaper article entitled "Shocking Murder," Meloy, a "bound Girl belonging [indentured] to Judge *Graff*, committed a most inhuman Murder of her new-born Babe." The article states that the "Circumstances, according to her own Confession, are too shocking to relate." Based on court records, this report does not appear to be a fabrication. Meloy beat and tore the baby's face, broke the jaw, and then shoved her fist into the infant's mouth. Although Meloy's case was not tried until August 1809, Snyder was undoubtedly aware of the pending charges against her while he was examining the petition for Susanna's clemency.

Moreover, the appearance of Mary Meloy's name in newspapers at the same time may have crystallized in the public's mind that a crime wave was afoot. In addition to Meloy, the May 1809 newspapers reported that Elizabeth Moore, a black slave, was found guilty of murder in the deaths of her two children. Then another slave, John Charles, was convicted of murdering his master. Although Elizabeth Moore was to be hanged for murder, her race disqualified her as the target to use as an example. Officials needed a white woman, one with whom the majority of Pennsylvania's female citizenry could identify. Susanna Cox was the perfect scapegoat.

Several factors made Susanna an easier target than Mary Meloy. One was her age. Mary Meloy was sixteen, a point newspaper articles emphasized consistently. Some stressed Meloy's youth by prefacing "sixteen" with the word "only." Although youth did not prohibit capital punishment in an age of changing attitudes, it undoubtedly invoked more sympathy.

Meloy also had an interesting defense. She said she was "moved and seduced by the instigation of the Devil." In a religious society, this defense elicited even more sympathy for the girl. She was not in control of her actions, and a female her age could not be expected to battle the Devil and emerge victorious.

While the prosecution at the Cox trial stressed the circumstances surrounding a previous pregnancy, thereby casting doubt about Susanna's morality, the Maryland article about Meloy emphasized she "has been generally of good Behaviour."

Another factor may have figured largely into Meloy's evasion of the hangman's noose. She was indentured to a judge who undoubtedly had influence within the legal system. He could assist Meloy in her defense. If he cared at all for his young charge, his presence would carry considerable weight in the courtroom. While Jacob Geehr spoke well of Susanna, he certainly lacked the legal savvy to launch a defense on her behalf.

Perhaps the most important element was that Mary Meloy spoke English, while Susanna probably knew little or none. This gave Meloy an edge, for she could plead her own case, beg for her life, and throw herself on the mercy of the court. Unlike Meloy, Susanna was unable to articulate her actions and feelings clearly, had anyone allowed her to defend herself. Then, too, Susanna may not have thought about pleading for mercy. Her parents had all but given her away, and the father of her child had abandoned his responsibilities to her and the infant. Her feelings of self-worth were probably so low, she viewed herself as a throw-away. Moreover, Susanna may have thought the court would not sentence her to death because she believed her baby was born dead.

As it happened, Susanna paid for a crime she may not have committed, simply because a scapegoat was needed to stop a wave of murders in the community. In all, Mary Meloy may have sealed Susanna Cox's fate.

Sometime on or before May 15, 1809, Susanna Cox received word that Governor Snyder would not commute the death sentence. Richards referenced the May 9 death warrant and quoted the brief note accompanying it:

> The Governor this day took into consideration the case of Susanna Cox, now under sentence of death for murder in the first degree, confined in the jail of the County of Berks of which crime she was convicted.

Along with the letter of transmittal, the warrant was delivered to Sheriff George Marx, who in turn read it to the prisoner. It was decided. The governor had taken Susanna's case into account; she was to be hanged on June 10, 1809, between the hours of 10:00 A.M. and 2:00 P.M. at the usual place of execution.

The Pennsylvania State Archives houses a letter from Marx to Nathaniel Brittan Boileau, the Snyder-appointed Secretary of the Commonwealth. Marx addressed the letter to "B. Boileau, Esq." and dated it "May 15, 1809." It read simply:

> A warrant for the execution of the Sentence upon Susanna Cox now confined in the jail of this County under sentence of death for murder in the first degree, has been duly received. I have agreeiably [sic] to my instructions communicated the same to the prisoner and shall also without delay take such measures as will eventually lead to the fulfillment of the duties enjoined on me in this important case.

Contemporary accounts reported that Susanna confessed when Marx read the death warrant to her. A brief paragraph claiming she confessed, in fact, followed the notice about the death warrant in *Der Readinger Adler* (*The Reading Eagle*). This assumption may have been added by a newspaper reporter, eager to point to her guilt. No evidence indicates this is true, and research strongly suggests it was pure fabrication by an anonymous author. Rather than confessing in May, Susanna maintained her innocence almost until the end. The actual confession was dated June 8, two days before her death.

In addition to his jailkeeping duties, Marx performed several more solemn rites. After receipt of the death warrant, it fell to him to inform the public of the impending execution. Susanna would serve as an example to other young women. Awareness of the hanging would indoctrinate people with lessons in morality. The notice of the death warrant from Governor Snyder was printed in the May 16, 1809, issue of the *Adler* newspaper. Presumably, Marx's office sent the notice to the editor.

After informing the public about the death warrant, Marx then placed a proclamation in three successive issues of the *Adler*; it appeared weekly from May 23 through June 6. The proclamation announced the time and the place of the execution and requested the presence of all necessary officials. In a time when personal stories rarely appeared on a newspaper's front page and many stories of interest were granted no space at all, the upcoming execution of Susanna Cox commanded front-page coverage. Marx's proclamation, translated from German, reads:

Notice is hereby given to all the Justices of the Peace, the Coroner, the Constables and to all other civil officers in the County of Berks that they and each of them have to appear in the Borough of Reading, in said county, on Saturday the tenth day of June next, then and there to assist the Sheriff of said County in preserving the peace and good order during the execution of a certain Susanna Cox, who at present is a prisoner in the common jail of the said County and is to be executed on said day at the ordinary place of execution.

Given under my hand the 19th day of May in the year of our Lord one thousand eight hundred and nine and in the thirty-third year of the Independence of America.

Marx had yet one other duty to perform. He would oversee the building of the gallows.

13

CONFESSION

The clergy oft did visit her
In her repentant state,
For earnestly she penance did,
Preparing for her fate.

—"A NEW DIRGE CONTAINING THE HISTORY OF SUSANNA COX"

After her sentencing on April 7, Susanna Cox was returned to her ward in the jail. While Marx prepared the gallows, Susanna prepared for death. As with the courts, protocol within prisons and jails was evolving. In 1809, the only regulations that mattered were those instituted by the local sheriff and jailer, in this case Marx and the undersheriff, Daniel Kerper. One of the few pleasures the inmates of the Reading jail could look forward to was the arrival of visitors. At Kerper's discretion, visitors were allowed to come and go as they wished. Although no mention is made of visitation by the Cox family, it is possible they came.

The curious, too, were allowed to visit. Sometimes they badgered the condemned, not only for a confession, but for the purpose of gossip. Hannah Ocuish, the previously mentioned twelve-year-old murderess, was continuously besieged by visitors who wanted her confession. Others merely wanted to torment her. Ocuish was often reduced to tears when visitors reminded her that death was near.

Susanna was visited regularly by a group of church women who were making her execution costume, which also would serve as her burial gown. Reportedly, it was the only new dress Susanna ever wore.

Baum mentioned in his testimony that he visited Susanna immediately following her arrest. Another person who visited Susanna from the outset was the local German Reformed minister, Philip Reinhold Pauli. The aged minister did not judge whether Susanna was guilty or innocent. His only concern was for the state of her soul. Both his influence and Susanna's upbringing within a Pennsylvania German community, heavily saturated with Christian mores, probably made Susanna concerned for her soul as well.

Pauli's calming presence toward the end of Susanna's life was fortunate. The reverend was a former Hessian who was captured aboard the British ship *Jason* in 1779. He was imprisoned at Rutland, Massachusetts, and remained in the newly founded country after the Revolution. In 1789, at the age of forty-seven, Pauli became an ordained minister of the Reformed Church, at the same time receiving an honorary degree from the University of Pennsylvania. In 1793, he transferred to Reading, where in addition to his pastoral duties, he conducted a select Latin and French school. Later, after Pauli narrowly escaped murder at the hands of insane Berks County farmer John Schild, Pauli visited Schild in jail every day following his conviction and imprisonment in 1812. It can be presumed he did the same for Susanna Cox.

Religion in the daily lives of German-speaking communities in Pennsylvania is evident in printed books, almanacs, poetry, musical lyrics, and written records. Moralistic broadsides were widely circulated. They included stories about Adam and Eve, Joseph, and Jesus's longings, as well as prayers and warnings about working on Sundays. A broadside entitled *Neue Jerusalem* ("New Jerusalem"), popularized by G. S. Peters (1793–1847) in the 1820s, shows individuals walking three paths. The most unfortunate souls take the easy path and meet their doom at the hands of a fiercely depicted devil. The center road illustrates an uphill climb, but the road eventually turns down toward the Grim Reaper, where sojourners fall into Hell. The steepest and most narrow path shows the few righteous individuals climbing toward Heaven. Moral lessons such as this were common throughout the Pennsylvania German cultural landscape, repeatedly expressed visually and verbally. Despite Susanna's ignorance, she would have been influenced by these constant reminders of the basic principles of moral behavior. She undoubtedly understood right from wrong, for she concealed her pregnancy and the birth of her son for fear of losing her job.

Beyond laws that dealt with societal order and human decency, another issue caused Pauli to play a crucial role in Susanna's final days—saving her soul. As it happened, this was not an altogether simple task.

In order to be saved according to Pauli, Susanna had to confess to the crime. Susanna wanted to go to Heaven, but at this point she was incessantly reminded her soul was sure to burn in Hell because of the crime she was accused of committing. She would have believed this with all her heart, so Pauli was her only hope. His intentions were beyond reproach. He wanted a heavenly reward for Susanna. As far as Pauli was concerned, the only way for him to ensure her salvation was through her confession and prayer. Susanna Cox was under tremendous pressure to confess for yet another reason. Her confession would ease the conscience of the citizens of Reading and Berks County. After all, hanging an innocent girl was tantamount to murder. With no offer of clemency, Susanna had nowhere to turn. Pauli offered a rewarding afterlife, so why not confess?

Contrary to accounts published at the time, no hard evidence exists that Susanna ever did confess. Franks's words in the court docket state she died "penitent," meaning he believed she confessed. An eight-page printed pamphlet, called in English "The Last Words and Dying Confession of Susanna Cox" and dated June 8, 1809, further suggests she confessed. But Susanna, who could neither read nor write, did not author the "confession."

Regardless, the day before her execution, Reverend Pauli administered communion and prayed with Susanna. At the time and place of the execution, it was Pauli who delivered one last prayer. His presence in her hour of need offered fatherly comfort to the doomed girl.

In 1967, sociologists Negley K. Teeters and Jack H. Hedblom estimated some sixteen thousand men, women, and children had been executed by rope in America. These figures certainly call into question the deterrent value of hanging convicted criminals. But rather than serving as a deterrent to crime, this simple young woman altered the course of public execution in Pennsylvania—a small step in liberalizing laws concerning capital punishment, but a giant step in providing a modicum of dignity for the doomed.

14

I POOR WRETCH

Just as the clock did strike elev'n,
She straightways from the jail
Was led to where the gallows stood,
Oh lamentable Tale!

—"A NEW DIRGE CONTAINING THE HISTORY OF SUSANNA COX"

While Reverend Pauli tended to Susanna's soul, George Marx and Daniel Kerper built an amazingly simple apparatus that would bring about her death. The typical gallows reflected in American folklore, films, and popular culture is an elaborate contrivance with thirteen steps leading to a platform in which a swinging trapdoor is set. The condemned is led or dragged up the steps and made to stand on the platform as a noose is placed around the neck. The preacher stands nearby, tightly gripping his holy book. Eventually, the trapdoor springs open and the prisoner is either hanged or released from that ghastly fate with a well-timed rifle shot by a nearby comrade.

At the reenactment of the Susanna Cox hanging at the Kutztown Folk Festival, the trapdoor gallows is used. The Kutztown gallows is modeled after an authentic one at the Mercer Museum in Doylestown, Pennsylvania. The reenactment represents an authentic hanging; however, it is not an accurate portrayal of Susanna Cox's hanging.

Hanging has been a lasting and prolific form of execution for one reason—it is cheap. In the seventeenth century and early into the eighteenth century, official hangings required a tree, a rope, and a ladder. The ladder was propped against the tree and the condemned, with noose around the neck, was forced to climb it while the other end was fastened to a branch. Then the unfortunate soul was "turned off." This meant the executioner quickly turned the ladder away, jerking support from under the doomed person's feet. The condemned would either be left to strangle, or more mercifully, die immediately from a broken neck. This method proved both simple and inexpensive, but there was one problem. Turning off did not always work. Some condemned would grab the ladder with their legs for support or they would never let go in the first place. Although there is evidence that a scaffold-type gallows with the trapdoor existed as early as 1694, turning off was still the more common method of hanging in the seventeenth and early eighteenth centuries.

By the later eighteenth century, turning off gave way to a more effective method of execution. The condemned stood in a horse-drawn cart placed underneath a gallows, which consisted of two posts with a crossbeam. The two posts were placed far enough apart that the doomed had no hope of grasping them for support. At the designated time, the horse was led away, leaving the person to either strangle slowly or die quickly with a broken neck. This was the method used for hanging Susanna Cox.

History's best witness of Susanna's execution was provided by Jacob Pile, who was an eleven-year-old boy at the time. Sixty-six years after the hanging, Pile, an attorney and teacher among other professions, wrote a letter to the *Times* (probably the *Reading Times and Dispatch*), describing the execution in as much detail as he could remember. Entitled "How Susanna Cox was Hung," the letter, presumably printed in the *Times* from the original, was found in A. S. Jones's scrapbook at the Historical Society of Berks County.

Pile's father, Daniel Pile, who lived near Douglassville, decided to take some of his children and neighbors to the Cox hanging in the hopes the execution might "prove a life long remembrance to them." Pile loaded his wagon, taking along a tenant farmer and an elderly Revolutionary War widow, Mrs. Hertlein. According to the younger Pile, his father proceeded along the road to Gallows Hill in Reading. Daniel had attended past executions, so he staked out a spot within view of the gallows. Jacob estimated the time was about 10:00 or 10:30 in the morning.

In his letter, Jacob failed to mention some facts about this day. In 1812, fewer than four thousand people resided in Reading. On June 10, 1809, however, there were reportedly fifteen thousand to twenty thousand people in town. Some traveled seventy miles to witness the hanging. Business boomed. Taverns and inns overflowed with patrons. Churches filled with prayer groups. Boys hawked Cox-related broadsides and pamphlets, shouting loudly they had Susanna's true confession, as they wound their way through crowds. Print shops and booksellers also conducted a brisk business selling these items. Reading would rarely have such an air of excitement. Although the purpose of public executions was to serve as a sober moral lesson, a surreal atmosphere took hold on the town.

Perhaps because young Pile was so near the execution site, he neglected to describe the initial procession in which Susanna was led to the gallows. The multitudes gathered along the condemned's route in advance of the hanging. In this fashion, more would be able to witness her long walk. Like the hanging, Susanna's walk to her execution was designed for the greatest impact. Public executions reminded onlookers, especially children, to walk the straight and narrow.

Led by Capt. Nicholas Lutz, the procession began at the jail with a military guard. The captain, 1st Lt. Peter Heller, and a few others would have been on horseback. The remainder of the guard was on foot. Lutz, Heller, and their men were, in turn, followed by the sheriff and other officials. A one-horse cart, driven by the executioner and containing Susanna's coffin, followed the officiating group. The cart was followed by the doomed Susanna on foot.

If the sad sight of Susanna Cox being forced to walk the length of Penn Street following her own coffin was not a deterrent for future criminals, they were hardened indeed. Newspaper accounts stated many spectators shed tears on her behalf. Accounts reported she stopped at a water pump to quench her thirst one last time.

Meanwhile, people called out encouraging words as she passed. The aged Reverend Pauli walked with Susanna, supporting her, providing what comfort he could.

The defense attorneys also walked in the procession, according to J. Bennett Nolan in *The Smith Family of Pennsylvania*. This is a possibility, but no eyewitness confirmed this claim. Furthermore, while family members were allowed to escort the condemned, no firsthand account mentioned that Susanna's family walked in the procession that day. Her sister, Barbara Katzenmoyer, and her husband Peter, however, were present at the hanging.

Upon the arrival of the Pile family at Gallows Hill, young Jacob observed the gallows, which had been constructed earlier and staged by either Sheriff Marx or Undersheriff Kerper. Pile described the gallows as "bright sawed scantling about five inches square and eleven feet high and wide enough for a wagon to pass through." He then went on to describe the arrival of the guards. "They formed a circle about eighty yards in diameter around the gallows." This would ensure that Susanna did not try to flee, or more importantly, the vast crowd would keep their distance and not help her escape. Crowds at public executions occasionally became so unruly and ill-behaved that guards were necessary to ensure order as well as dignity.

Pile also noted the church bells began to toll as "an announcement of their coming." He stated that when she came into view, Susanna was accompanied by two ministers, one on either side. The other minister may have been Pauli's son, William, who was training with his father. Pile noted both preachers donned black garb, while Susanna wore a white dress adorned with a broad black ribbon at her waist. It was at this point that Pile noticed the executioner opening Susanna's coffin to take out a bottle and take a "heavy draught." While the executioner was imbibing, the ministers performed their devotions. Of course, much of these proceedings were unheard and unseen by thousands because of the sheer size of the crowd.

It was traditional at momentous events for participants and attendees to sing an appropriate hymn. The hanging of Susanna Cox was no exception. It was written that Susanna selected the hymn, but more than likely Pauli chose the hymn for her. Regard-less, all joined in and sang, in German, the penitence hymn which begins "Ich armer Mensch:"

Ich armer Mensch, ich armer Sünder,
Steh hier vor Gottes Angesicht.
Ach Gott!, ach Gott! verfahr gelinder,
Und geh nicht mit mir ins Gericht.
Erbarme dich, erbarme dich,
Gott, mein Erbarmer, über mich!

A non-rhyming English translation of the first stanza reads:

I poor wretch, I poor sinner,
Stand here before God's sight;
Oh God! Oh God! Show mercy,
And judge me not,
Take pity, Thou take pity,
God, take pity on me.

Susanna probably sang along quietly. It was common for pris-oners to memorize short verses or poems they would convey to the crowd. It was also common for the condemned to express remorse or warn onlookers not to follow in their footsteps. Susanna was allowed to speak if she wished, but Pile, whose proximity to the hanging would have enabled him to hear, made no mention of her having uttered any words. Two other witnesses gave their accounts of the event to newspapers, and neither mentioned her speaking. Susanna's apparent acceptance of her fate did not go unnoticed by Pile. He mentioned how calm and submissive she seemed despite being moments from death.

After a fashion, preparations got underway. Today, these prepa-rations seem inept, and if not for the circumstances, comical. The gallows were too tall and the rope was not long enough to reach from Susanna to the crossbeam. The officials, caught unawares, quickly remedied the situation. They placed Susanna's coffin cross-wise on the side rails of the cart to gain additional height. Susanna was then lifted onto the cart by two men, who then lifted her again and stood her on her coffin. In a solemn affair already gone wrong,

Pile described how all three in the cart were nearly toppled when the horse suddenly lurched. Meanwhile, other officials busied themselves procuring other objects on which to stand so they could reach the top of the gallows to fasten the rope, which was not yet in place. Through all of these last-minute adjustments, Pile noticed Susanna standing "pensive and alone on her coffin under the gallows."

Although the executioner likely had a hood to hide his face, Pile made no mention of this fact. Executioners had an unpopular job; they were at times blackmailed to perform the task. A disguise was a proper safety measure. Sometimes instead of wearing a hood, executioners wore masks, often grotesque ones that drew attention from their recognizable physical features. Some simply blackened their faces.

At many executions, the condemned wore a black or white hood. Louis Richards wrote that both Susanna and her executioner were hooded. It would have been common practice.

Mary Dyer, a Quaker who was to be hanged in 1659 by Puritans, was given a handkerchief to cover her face. The head covering became unnecessary in that instance, because her life was spared. (A year later, she was hanged in Massachusetts for "Quakerism.") In another instance, in 1821, Stephen Clark, a young arsonist in Salem, Massachusetts, had a "death cap" pulled over the face at his execution. "Black Jack" Tom Ketchum, a well-known southwestern outlaw, had a hood placed over his head at his 1901 hanging in Clayton, New Mexico. The hoods were not only for the condemned, but for the audience as well. Hoods and death caps insulated spectators from the true hideousness of a ligature execution. In fact, because of the weight he gained while in prison, Black Jack's head was torn off during his hanging.

After all arrangements were made, Susanna's executioner took one side of the horse's reins while another official held the other side and together they drew the horse forward. Susanna was drawn from the coffin, and once the rope jolted at her weight, "the gallows quivered," said Pile. She twirled and swung to and fro.

"*Ey, du, Allmaechtiger Gott im Himmel!*" (Oh, Thou, Almighty God in Heaven!), Widow Hertlein exclaimed. Some contemporary accounts said it took several excruciating minutes for Susanna to

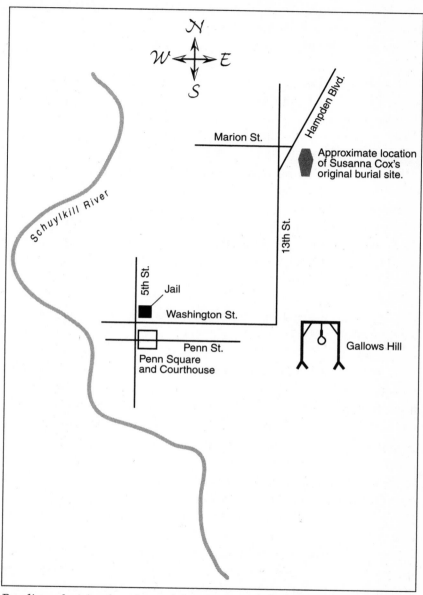

Reading, showing locations of the courthouse, jail, Gallows Hill, and the approximate spot where Susanna Cox was buried until 1905.

die. All told, it took fifteen to seventeen minutes from the time her foot support was withdrawn to the time her body was removed from the noose. Pile described the last moments of the hanging:

> Presently [Susanna's] hands, which she had kept erect, suddenly dropped, retaining her white handkerchief in them. The executioner, who was not the Sheriff, but some other man, then grasped her feet, raised them a little, and then gave her a jolt, for which, as I am told, he got a severe beating the next day by some citizens of Reading. Her head lay on her shoulder—I think on the right—while the rope was suspended on the opposite side, and her black slippers were down over her heels; but being tied over the instep, were prevented from falling off. After being thus suspended in the air for about fifteen minutes and having been the object of thousands of her fellow mortals, who gazed on her, I trust, with aching hearts and streaming eyes, the cart was then backed under and her lifeless body taken down, placed in her coffin and taken away.

Another eyewitness, Jacob Bright Hoff, then thirteen years old, corroborated much of Pile's story in his own account of the hanging. He was interviewed for an 1881 article, which celebrated his eighty-fifth year. Hoff added insights Pile did not provide. As far as is known, Hoff is the only identified contemporary to physically describe Susanna beyond Jacob Geehr's mention of her stout frame in his trial testimony. Hoff said Susanna was a pretty girl with black hair and black eyes. He also mentioned that it was Undersheriff Kerper who jumped into the cart, lifted Susanna, and fastened the end of the rope to the gallows.

Hoff added another startling detail. He said the noose was withdrawn from the folds of Susanna's clothing, where it had been concealed during the procession. Therefore, the noose was not in place awaiting Susanna's arrival at the gallows, but had been around her neck the entire time.

Hoff mentioned that Dr. Baum bled Susanna and pronounced her dead upon her removal from the gallows. This practice of bleeding the hanged was common at the time, because some persons revived, usually brain dead, after being nearly executed. In the parlance of the day, Susanna was bled to ensure her heart had stopped pumping.

After the hanging, the Piles, the Hoffs, and the rest of the crowd slowly returned to their homes, to churches for vigils, or to inns and taverns for heavy draughts themselves. Moral lessons were supposedly learned and remembered.

It was finally over for Susanna Cox. Her body was placed in her coffin and driven away by cart. Most records claim she was buried on the land of relatives. One account said six hundred people attended her burial. The most credible account states that Barbara and Peter Katzenmoyer retrieved the body and buried it. Some suggest it was Peter who drove the cart containing Susanna's coffin and cooling body away from Gallows Hill. If true, perhaps Barbara was with Cox as she took her final walk.

Susanna's sister and brother-in-law were local farmers who lived in what is now the Hampden Park area of Reading. It is believed sometime during the night, they buried Susanna in a field on the outskirts of the Katzenmoyer farm.

Stones were placed on Susanna's grave to conceal the location. Her body was then guarded for a time to prevent grave robbers from exhuming it. Richards stated this was a request made by Susanna herself, for she was concerned her body would be dissected. According to his account, Susanna's unmarked grave was near the spot in Reading where Thirteenth Street and Marion Street were eventually joined. An 1890s newspaper account said that people passing by wept at the sight of the unmarked grave twenty feet from the roadside, "where lay the body of Susanna Cox."

15

A FINAL JOLT

She was then made to undergo
The punishment of death;
Scarce sev'nteen minutes had expired,
When she resigned her breath.

—"A NEW DIRGE CONTAINING THE HISTORY OF SUSANNA COX"

As Susanna's body was removed from Gallows Hill, anger about her execution, or the way it was conducted, suddenly turned violent. Newspaper and eyewitness accounts reported that the crowd initially remained orderly and dignified, despite some animosity towards the system that condemned Susanna. But emotion was running high and an easy target was available—the executioner. Some in the crowd vented their anger and frustration, and without warning turned on him.

Executioners in the Colonial Era and the Early Republic were not of a professional caste as they were in England. Often, American law enforcement officers were hard put to find someone willing to act as an executioner. In some states, such as Maryland, it was so difficult to find executioners that authorities gave death sentence reprieves to prisoners, should they be willing to put to death one of their peers. Whether a professional or not, executioners were never properly trained, as would later become standard.

In addition to ensuring the death of the prisoner, the executioner occasionally had other duties. For hangings, these included measuring the condemned for the length of rope necessary to truss and hang the doomed. Judging by Pile's account, no one measured Susanna. Binding the inmate would ensure limbs would not flail about—a distressing and shocking sight for onlookers. Thus, trussing kept the condemned in a neat bundle, making hanging more palatable. Pile did not mention if Susanna was trussed. He described no flailing about, only of the body swinging to and fro, so apparently she was bound. Because he described her hands dropping while still holding her handkerchief, she was probably bound at the waist with her elbows pinned to her sides.

At some point during the fifteen to seventeen minutes it took for Susanna to strangle, the executioner grasped her feet, raised them a little, and gave her a jolt. Some surmise this was an act of cruelty on his part. Others believe the executioner was trying to fix her shoes, which were about to drop. The latter seems unlikely because Pile stated the shoes were about to fall, but were saved from doing so by a strap over the instep. And surely Pile would have said the executioner merely fixed the shoes, instead of stating the executioner delivered a final jolt. The best explanation for the executioner's actions would be that his was an act of mercy. Unfortunately for Susanna, the knot did not break her neck. Instead she suffered the anguish of strangulation. The hangman may have decided to end Susanna's suffering.

Other instances of hangmen ending an execution quickly are known. In 1738, in Williamsburg, Virginia, Anthony Dittond was hanged by the same method as Susanna, a horse-drawn cart pulled from under a gallows. Like Susanna, his neck did not break from the drop. After three minutes of torment, the executioner jerked Dittond's legs in a similar fashion. That Susanna's executioner willingly, if not happily, delivered a death blow seems unlikely. After all, he took a swig of liquid courage to steel himself for the grisly task that lay ahead.

Contrary to popular belief, placing the knot of the noose properly on the neck so it will break is a false presumption. That executioners had extensive knowledge of this knot lore likewise appears to be untrue. Beliefs about knot placement survive from the seventeenth century, but insufficient evidence supports the idea that placing the knot under the ear caused instant death by breaking the spine. Too few cervical fractures confirm this theory. Instead, it was a matter of luck as to whether one's neck broke immediately. Susanna was unlucky, and she died slowly. It is possible that either the rope cut the blood flow to her brain or she was unable to breathe and quickly lost consciousness. If her blood flow was interrupted, this would have been the least painful manner of death, for she would lose consciousness without struggling for air. Asphyxiation would leave her writhing and gasping. Inevitably, her mouth and nose turned a deep purple and her eyes and tongue bulged. Such descriptions are one of the reasons hoods were supplied—to spare the audience from these horrific sights and to provide at least some dignity to the condemned. Convulsions spread throughout Susanna's body. She might have released her bowels and bladder. With one jerk of her feet, the executioner probably ended the humiliation, pain, and torment for her.

Despite the executioner's reasons and actions, justified or not, it would have served him well to retreat hastily from Reading. As it happened, the anonymous executioner was followed by Andrew McCoy, a well-known bully in Reading. McCoy overtook the executioner at Sixth Street and Penn Street and soundly beat the man, at which time the money reportedly flew from his pockets. Some called it his "blood money." The badly beaten executioner did not retrieve the money, but scurried off.

16

PEACE BE TO HER

*So that 10th of June, 1809, is the day whereof Berks
County used to think and weep.*

—A. E. WATROUS

Few of the thousands of people hanged legally in this country
have been immortalized. History and popular culture recall the
hangings of the Lincoln conspirators, convicted train robber "Black
Jack" Tom Ketchum, Clutter family murderers Perry Smith and
Richard Hickock of *In Cold Blood* infamy, and rapist-murderer
Rainey Bethea, who has the distinction of being the last person
publicly hanged in the United States in 1936. Surprisingly, Susanna
Cox, a simple Pennsylvania German girl, was not to be among the
forgotten. Her court docket includes the notations:

Respublica v. Susanna Cox
Indictment for Murder, returned by the Grand Inquest, a true
Bill . . . and now April Seventh AD. MDCCCIX, a Jury being
called came . . . twelve free honest and lawful men, who
being duly balloted sworn and affirmed tried and charged
respectively do say that the Prisoner Susanna Cox is Guilty of
Murder in the first degree in manner and form she stands

indicted. Sentence of the Court is that Susanna Cox be hanged by the neck until she be dead.

This was followed by:

On the 10th of June AD 1809, the prisoner was Executed, previous to which she confessed the murder and died penitent. Peace be to her. Memorandum by Mr. Franks.

After the hanging and the violence that ensued, Reading returned to normal. Sheriff Marx disassembled the gallows. It was common practice for sheriffs to sell pieces of the rope used to hang recently executed persons. The demand was so great for these souvenirs that people typically surged toward the gallows to obtain a part of the rope or death mask or whatever other items they could capture. Some folks placed lengths of the rope in a bottle by their doors to ward off evil spirits. Sections of the rope were also stuffed in the handles of farm implements to ensure bountiful crops. There is, however, no record of the stoic Marx or ambitious Kerper profiting from Susanna's death.

Newspaper articles issued immediately after Susanna's execution were plentiful. The Cox story was so popular, both English- and German-language papers carried the story. This was unusual in a time when papers focused more on international news, accompanied by advertisements, rather than sensational stories. Nonetheless, the Susanna Cox story could be found in multiple venues. Reprints of editorial pieces opposing her execution appeared as far north as Massachusetts. The July 5, 1809, issue of *The Centinel* of Gettysburg, Pennsylvania, reported the following:

Last Saturday the Execution of the unfortunate Susannah Cox took place. Never did Reading behold so numerous a collection of people. The taverns were all crouded [*sic*] the preceding evening and all night wagons loaded with people from the country, were passing through the streets, some coming upwards of 70 miles to see this truly unfortunate girl terminate here [*sic*] earthly existence; and from the ground occupied by the spectators (a number of them having placed themselves in sections, previously) on the hill, allowing each to take up one yard, the number rather exceeded twenty thousand. A little after eleven o'clock the mournful procession moved from the jail — the unfortunate girl with a wonderful serenity, intermixed with a smile in her countenance, walked straight up to the awful place of execution, on the commons, at the foot of the hill, supported and comforted by two Reverend Ministers, kneeled down as soon as arrived, and committed her last fervent prayer to an Almighty God and Redeemer, to whom she had, during her confinement (after the death warrant being read to her) most earnestly supplicated for mercy and forgiveness of sins and transgressions, with whom she had made her peace, & from whom, she assured, she, had received the comfort of his mercy and grace. She shortly after ascended the scaffold, willingly surrendering a body of sins for the satisfaction of the offended laws of the country, when she was launched into eternity without a struggle. The greatest decency was observed during the whole awful scene, and tears of sympathy were seen flowing spontaneously from the most numerous croud [*sic*] of spectators. It was indeed a day of sorrow.

Hence, the newspapers contributed to distortions in the Cox story. The above article was reprinted from a June 17, 1809, edition of Reading's *The Weekly Advertiser*. The paper suggested the entire affair was solemn and orderly, conveniently overlooking matters such as officials scrambling to adjust for the height of the gallows, the horse almost toppling Susanna and others from the cart, and Andrew McCoy beating the executioner. The papers probably intended to preserve Reading's dignity.

Although the article had fanciful parts, such as the scaffold and her "smiling countenance," the sentiment was real. Susanna Cox did not exactly become a nineteenth-century poster child for the argument against capital punishment or for judicial reform, but some felt her trial was too short and the evidence too flimsy. Conspiracy and cover-up theories gained momentum later in the century. These romanticized notions never died, for some believed and still believe influential people hastily ensured Susanna's removal. But the sensationalism of 1809 subsided. People involved in the case went on with their lives. After all, a country had to be built, an ominous embargo was in place, and people were debating the impact of Napoleon's quest for domination of Europe.

Life resumed as usual, except for President Judge John Spayd. Like the executioner, Spayd suffered outrage concerning Susanna's fate. Although popular versions of the Cox story hold Spayd resigned because of grief over the Cox sentence, Negley K. Teeters maintained Spayd's resignation at age forty-five may not have been a personal choice, but the result of public badgering. Teeter's scenario seems more likely given the lack of the judge's interest in Susanna Cox. As a result, Spayd may have felt the immediate effects of his failure to anticipate what became a long-lasting interest in Susanna Cox.

Spayd was again admitted to the bar in 1810, but that April, less than a year after Susanna was executed, he found himself on the defensive in the case of *Respublica versus John Spayd*. Unfortunately, no details of the case have been discovered, except that Samuel D. Franks was also involved.

But life went on for Spayd, too. His name appears frequently in contemporary articles and later history books about Pennsylvania. During the War of 1812, in 1814, he placed an advertisement in *The Weekly Advertiser* in which he asked residents to voluntarily surrender their firearms so that the weapons could be repaired and distributed among volunteers for the defense of Pennsylvania. On April 16, 1815, recognizing the need for cleaner and purer water in Reading, he organized the city's first water service, the Hampden Water Company. In a strange turn of events, during the formation of this company, he also became part owner of one of the Katzenmoyer houses.

In 1821, Spayd became a justice of the peace. The following year, however, he traveled to Philadelphia to seek surgical relief from a long illness. He died shortly after the operation on October 13, 1822.

Spayd was initially buried in the Reading Lutheran Graveyard, but his remains were eventually reinterred at Charles Evans Cemetery. The following is an excerpt from his obituary:

> To him justly belonged the high praise of having refuted by his life the numerous calumnies that have been propagated against his profession. Independent and upright, his whole career proved that a long course of successful practice at the bar, did not necessarily impair the sense of right and wrong; but that the most perfect candor and undeviating integrity were strictly compatible with the character of the *lawyer* and the *advocate*.
>
> As an advocate indeed, his manner was almost peculiar. Disdaining every thing like artifice or [technical] advantage, he looked to the merits of the case alone. Although profoundly versed in the laws of his country, he seemed ever to contend for *justice* rather than for *victory*. Hence his influence with the court and the jury was deservedly great.

Surprisingly, no mention was made of Spayd having served as a judge. Seemingly, he preferred this chapter in his life remain closed.

The theatrical Samuel D. Franks died young, but he lived fully. He was Second Lieutenant of Reading from September 1 to December 4, 1814. During the War of 1812, he became a major in a Berks County regiment of volunteers at Baltimore when that city was threatened by the British, although he saw no action.

Jacob Bright Hoff recounted an interesting anecdote regarding Franks:

> Anthony Morris, a rich young man, who lived in Philadelphia but spent his summers in Reading, had a duel in 1816 with Judge Franks about a young lady of this city. Franks was shot in the hip and he was carried in a blanket to a house on South Fifth street where John S. Pearson lives, where the doctors extracted the bullet. Morris thought he had killed him and ran off, and Franks married the girl. Her name was

May and she lived with her father on Penn street below the Eagle Office.

After this turmoil, Franks became a prothonotary and clerk of the quarter sessions in 1818. During this period, he found time to pursue his interest in the military, whereby he was elected major-general of the 6th Division Pennsylvania Militia. Franks also maintained a position as a president judge in Dauphin County until his forced resignation in 1830. He died a few months later at the age of forty-six.

Marks John Biddle, the eldest of Susanna's defense attorneys, became a prothonotary and a state senator. He is credited with introducing "stone coal," or anthracite, at the same time the first coal stove was introduced in Reading by William Stahle. Meanwhile, he was listed as a merchant on tax lists of the time. Seven years before his death in 1859, he was struck blind.

Charles Evans, also on the defense team, retired in 1828 after amassing a fortune. He eventually became known as Reading's first philanthropist. He founded Reading's Charles Evans Cemetery, still a stunning landmark. Evans died in 1847, one year after founding the cemetery.

Frederick Smith, the youngest of the defense attorneys, enjoyed a successful legal career. He became a deputy attorney general of Berks County and held that position from 1818 to 1821. Smith then served as Pennsylvania's attorney general from 1823 to 1828. His political aspirations did not end there. He later became an associate justice of the Supreme Court of Pennsylvania. He held that position from 1828 to 1830. In 1830, he died in Reading and according to his wishes, was buried next to his daughter, Mary Ann.

Smith remains the best known of the three defense attorneys, but not only because of his success in Pennsylvania's political and judicial system. The last documented indentured servant in Pennsylvania, and possibly in the United States, died in Reading in 1903. Margaret Quacco was a Creole who came to Reading from New Orleans in 1818 and was indentured to Smith for a time.

A court case brought against Smith and his wife, Catharine, suggests the Smiths cared little about the welfare of their servants.

The Smiths are listed as defendants against the commonwealth in the quarter sessions minutes of 1805 to 1809. The records say:

> Sent to the Grand Jury August 2nd 1808, on complaint of John Jacob Fisher against his master and mistress the defendants for ill treatment. Upon a hearing of the parties the court direct that Frederick Smith, Esq. give security in 100 dollars on conditi[on] that Catharine Smith be of the peace as towards John Jacob Fisher till next sessions.

Furthermore, while the Pennsylvania Legislature passed laws concerning the gradual abolition of slavery in 1780, one record finds that Smith and others did not quite follow the letter of the law. Addressed to Smith by J. H. Baker of Franklin Court and dated March 11, 1814, the letter reads:

> Your brother Jacob called on me about your blk girl to sell for you. My commission in selling is Ten pds. I will give you Peter for your girl. He has 8 years to serve from the 2d inst. My price for him is $260. I have bought him new clothes. He is a good Coachman Waiter Gardener & Cook & can Bake. He is Sober, industrious, Good Natured, Willing & Obliging. I have for sale a Blk Girl about 20 years old & 10 to serve. She is a good Cook, can Bake, Wash, Iron, Milk, Sew, Knit & Weave, Good Natured, Willing & obliging.

The Smiths' actions reaffirm that, although indentured servants had certain rights, they were of a different caste than those who made a living through business, farming, or trade. Perhaps this attitude towards indentured servants influenced Smith's weak defense of Susanna Cox.

Many treasures are stored at the Historical Society of Berks County, one of which is a box containing an extensive log of Smith's cases before the Sessions of Oyer and Terminer. Thumbing through these notes, one expects to see Smith's mention of Susanna Cox. Surprisingly, despite his careful notes concerning numerous other cases and his compensation for his involvement in them, Smith did not mention her. At the end of his records pertaining to the April 1809 Oyer and Terminer Session, where Susanna's case would fall, Smith ended abruptly, leaving a near-blank page. The possibility exists that, if Smith defended Susanna pro bono, he did not record it, for many of his entries contained notes concerning receipt of fees. The possibility also exists that Susanna Cox did not matter to him. Smith simply dismissed her and resumed his busy life as did others.

Of the three lawmen, Marx, Nagle, and Kerper, the least is known about Marx. The memory of Marx remains mostly in reference to the story of Susanna Cox. The Nagle name is familiar, even now, because of a proud heritage of the family's involvement in the Revolutionary War and the many civil service offices held by Nagle and his son, Peter Nagle Jr. The lovely old Yellow House, which Nagle Jr. managed, and eventually owned, is still in operation as a hotel and restaurant renowned for fine dining. Not far from the Schneider–Geehr farm, it stands at a crossroads in Yellow House, a charming hamlet that can hardly be called a town, but simply a quaint corner of the beautiful Oley Valley.

Daniel Kerper eventually became the sheriff of Reading for two short terms. The first term, 1812 to 1814, began soon after the Cox tragedy, when Marx began supporting efforts leading up to the War of 1812. In 1815, Kerper became a member of the Assembly of Berks County. He became sheriff again from 1824 to 1826.

Like Marx, Dr. John Christian Baum seems to have disappeared from public record, except for a mention under estate administration records titled "Baum, John C. MD Reading." His estate was settled January 24, 1821. His wife Marian and son George were listed as benefactors.

Just as his grandfather proudly served during the Revolution, Dr. John Bodo Otto served his country in the War of 1812 as a surgeon for the 2nd Regiment. While some sources say he was not as ambitious as his grandfather, Otto was known as a kind man and a good doctor. The news of his death traveled to Clearfield, Pennsylvania, where the *Clearfield Republican* reported on August 11, 1858, "one of the oldest citizens of Reading, Pa., died a few days ago." His death obviously touched others beyond the boundaries of Berks County.

Rev. Philip Reinhold Pauli, who consistently demonstrated kindness to Susanna, died in 1815 at the age of sixty-six. He was the last Reformed minister of Reading to serve during the eighteenth century. Pauli's son, William, who may have been the second pastor reported at Susanna's side at the hanging, succeeded his father in Reading and served the Reformed congregation until 1842.

Jacob Geehr died in 1853 at the age of seventy-three, but his wife, Esther died in 1819 when she was only thirty-six. They had one more child after the Cox episode. Sara was born to them on January 16, 1810, but she died eleven days later. The Geehrs are buried in the Schneider family cemetery on the Schneider–Geehr farm.

Simon Snyder remained governor until 1817. The following year, he was elected to the U.S. Senate, but died in 1819 before he could serve. He is buried in the Sharon Lutheran Church Cemetery in Selinsgrove. Although it was Frederick Smith who encouraged John Spayd to run against Snyder in the 1808 gubernatorial elections, Snyder's son, Henry, married Smith's daughter, Mary, in 1828. The young couple then lived in Snyder's old stone mansion in Selinsgrove.

As Reading grew and changed, the city maintained a tightly knit community atmosphere. Looking back to the first decade of the nineteenth century, its early citizens included a small group of men who controlled much of what transpired in politics, city and business development, enforcement of the law, and social structure. Many of the same men involved in the Cox case were responsible for the growth of Reading. Their industrious activities, which began before the Cox trial, continued long after Susanna's moment of infamy.

Charles Evans, John Spayd, and Samuel D. Franks worked together on at least one more case involving murder—the previously mentioned John Schild case. After Schild's murderous rampage on August 12, 1812, Daniel Kerper, then the sheriff, arrested Schild. On November 1, 1812, Schild's court hearing began. Despite being caught red-handed, Schild was given a five-day trial with two days of testimony that included fifteen witnesses for the commonwealth and thirty on his behalf. By contrast, Susanna Cox had only one witness for her defense against three for the commonwealth. Unlike Susanna, Schild spoke in his own defense.

It did him no good. On November 5, 1812, John Schild was declared guilty of murder in the first degree. On November 9, the court asked him if he had anything to say for himself, which gave his counsel pause. Spayd and Evans asked the court for more time and their request was granted. Although the efforts of the lawyers seemed more strenuous on Schild's behalf than they were on Susanna's, Schild was executed on June 20, 1813.

Despite the ghastly nature of the Schild murder, it was Susanna's story that captured and held the attention of Pennsylvanians. As evidence of this, broadsides of the Schild murder were printed, but they enjoyed nowhere near the popularity of Susanna Cox broadsides. To date, only one edition of Schild's broadside has surfaced, whereas more than eighty editions of Susanna's broadside are known.

As time passed, Gallows Hill became part of Reading's City Park, now a beautiful, sprawling hillside covered with memorials. There are no monuments commemorating its original use as Gallows Hill. In 1821, the reservoir in City Park was put into service, and now the park is a tribute to Reading's citizens who served in America's wars. In 1840, the dirt road where Susanna walked to her death was covered with gravel. Also that year, the courthouse in which Susanna was found guilty was demolished because it blocked the view of Mount Penn. The jail followed suit in 1910.

The house where Susanna once worked stands on the Charles Hetrick farm east of Reading. The private farm is still in operation, but the washhouse where Susanna allegedly hid the infant's body is now a pile of foundation stones. Out of concerns for safety, a member of Hetrick's family demolished the ground-level room after discovering children playing in the ruins.

Monocacy Creek, the little brook that babbles pleasantly nearby, enables one to momentarily forget the tragedy that occurred here. The washhouse remains are more than the few steps from the main house as Jacob Geehr mentioned in his testimony. The family dwelling has undergone several renovations since 1809. The Schneider family cemetery is easily visible from the house, where generations of Schneiders, Geehrs, and others are buried. Some of the graves are marked by veterans groups as the resting places of Revolutionary War heroes. Many of the gravestones rest in neat piles atop the stone wall.

The Hetrick family is well-versed in the legend of Susanna Cox. Charles Hetrick's version of the story, as it was told to him, states Jacob Geehr was the father of Cox's baby. Similar to many residents of Berks County today, Hetrick questions Susanna's guilt. Either way, many locals hold the opinion that someone rich and powerful hurried the trial and execution, and more importantly, they believe Susanna should not have been hanged.

According to some folks, a door opens occasionally in the Hetrick home—by itself. A light footstep is heard when no one is there. Hetrick feels Susanna Cox is making her presence known and believes that until justice is done, Susanna's spirit will linger. Perhaps Franks's statement, "Peace be to her," was not enough to make it so.

Louis Richards's scrapbook, preserved at the Historical Society of Berks County, contains a small article from the *Reading Times and Dispatch*, dated May 19, 1905: "The bones of [a] woman hanged nearly 100 years ago for the killing of a child are unearthed in excavation operations on the Pricetown road." A handwritten notation on the page states "near Third and Marion Streets." No one knows what became of Susanna's skeletal remains. Neither her bones, nor those of any Jane Doe from 1905, were interred at Charles Evans Cemetery, unlike the remains of so many involved in her trial. Just as the final resting place of the baby's body is a mystery, so is the final resting place of Susanna Cox.

But Susanna's story by no means ended with her death. As those involved in her conviction moved on with their lives, Susanna's story assumed a life of its own. Her death opened new chapters with the immensely popular German-language ballad that lasted beyond all expectations.

17

THE PRINTERS OF EXETER TOWNSHIP

She bade them learn a lesson from
Her sad experience then
And hearken to the voice of God
And not to words of men.

—"A TALE OF SORROW," TRANSLATION BY FRANK B. COPP
OF THE BALLAD OF SUSANNA COX

Just days before Susanna Cox was hanged in Reading, the slaves Elizabeth Moore and John Charles were hanged in York, Pennsylvania. The murders that led to Moore's and Charles's executions, more sordid than that of the Cox case, warranted at least two editions of broadsides. Circulated throughout southeast Pennsylvania, these broadsides detail a convoluted tale of how Moore poisoned her young son and smothered her infant daughter. Almost as a footnote, the same broadside tells how John Charles murdered his master, Henrich Jung. The broadside that resulted from the executions of Moore and Charles was merely sensational journalism, not a moralistic lesson. Susanna Cox's best-known broadside, however, contains a popular ballad that outlines her story concurrently laced with moralistic overtones.

The widely distributed Cox broadside suggests the story endured throughout two centuries of Pennsylvania folklore because of its celebrated ballad. Thus, the Cox broadside kept her story alive while the tales of others who suffered the same fate faded from memory.

Importantly, the Cox ballad might not have been widely known had it not been for printers in southeast Pennsylvania who published in German. Prior to the Revolution, Philadelphia became the center of printing in America. Because Philadelphia was surrounded by large German-speaking populations, about half of what Philadelphia printers produced were German-language or bilingual publications. The most well-known of the early Philadelphia printers, of course, was Benjamin Franklin. Keenly aware of the German-speaking market, he printed in English and German.

Following the Revolution, numerous printing establishments popped up in towns distant from Philadelphia, so by 1788, Reading had its own printers. Although most Reading printers eventually changed from German to English or bilingual publications, the shift was gradual. For decades throughout the nineteenth century and into the twentieth century, Reading printers continued to publish German-language newspapers, books, almanacs, and broadsides. Long after Susanna Cox was executed, many Pennsylvania newspaper readers, especially subscribers in rural areas, still spoke the Pennsylvania Dutch dialect and they read High German. Of special interest, several of these German-language printers came to Reading from nearby Exeter Township, where the Cox story unfolded.

About 1794 or 1795, Daniel Schneider's cousins—brothers John Schneider (b. 1747) and Jacob Schneider (1763–ca. 1830)—along with Franz Ritter (1741–1825), built a printing press in Exeter Township. In 1796, the Schneider brothers and Ritter moved the press to Reading where Jacob Schneider and a man named George D. Gerrish began printing the German-language newspaper *Der Readinger Adler*, often referred to as the "Bible of Berks County." In 1804, Franz Ritter's son, John (1779–1851), took over the business, turning it into a highly successful enterprise. The Ritter and Schneider families intermarried several times. For example, Franz Ritter married Barbara Schneider (1745–1816), the older sister of John and Jacob Schneider. Also, John Schneider married a sister of Franz Ritter.

The Ritters and Schneiders counted yet another printer among their clan. The parents of Barbara, John, and Jacob Schneider were

Peter Schneider (1723–96) and Eva Appolonia Jungman (1721–99). Eva Appolonia was the aunt of Reading's first postmaster, Gottlob Jungman (ca. 1757–1833). As a young man prior to moving to Reading, Gottlob Jungman taught at Schneider's schoolhouse in Exeter Township. He began printing in Reading about 1789, and by 1793, he controlled the printing market in the town, until May 1796 when Jacob Schneider and George D. Gerrish established the *Adler*.

Importantly, Daniel Schneider, the same Daniel who owned the Schneider–Geehr farm where Susanna worked, was Peter Schneider's nephew. This close relationship to families having roots in the vicinity of the Cox tragedy probably prompted John Ritter, proprietor of the *Adler*, to publish broadsides about Susanna, as well as notices in his newspaper concerning developments in her case. He intimately knew the families involved, because he and Esther Geehr were second cousins. Also, Ritter was a shrewd businessman. He undoubtedly recognized an obvious business opportunity. He realized the town of Reading would swell with crowds coming to witness Susanna's hanging.

Almost immediately upon learning Susanna's death sentence was final, Ritter published a German-language broadside that contained three "rhymes." This broadside was not the well-known ballad that appeared on subsequent broadsides. It was unlike most poems on Pennsylvania German broadsides, which were often written in doggerel verse that can be described as generic, dry, and uninspiring. The rhymes on this earliest-known broadside concerning Susanna Cox, however, reflect the emotions of the moment.

The main headline of this important German-language broadside reads, "*Reime*" ("Rhymes"). The subhead and the three poems that follow indicate the broadside was published after Susanna learned her date of execution and before she was hanged. Thus, this broadside was published after May 16, 1809, and before June 10, the day of the hanging.

According to the imprint, Ritter published "*Reime*" at the request of an anonymous author. The author described in the first poem what he believed Susanna must have felt at the moment she heard straight from the sheriff's mouth that the date of execution was fixed. In the first stanza, the tone of shocking finality is expressed with simple words.

> *Eilend's kommt heran die Stunde,*
> *Da man mir das Leben nimmt.*

> *In haste comes herein the hour,*
> *When they end life for me.*

The sentiment is repeated as if in disbelief.

> *Junius, der zehnte Tag,*
> *Nimmt man mir das Leben ab.*

> *On the tenth day of June,*
> *They take from me my life.*

This horror, expressed from the first-person point-of-view, is followed by expressions of remorse and a plea to God for mercy and comfort. The fourth stanza describes an understandable fear of the anquish of death. Then, among all Susanna Cox broadsides, the fifth stanza contains a passage that comes closest to a confession. Here, Susanna admits to breaking the sixth and seventh commandments, "thou shalt not kill" and "thou shalt not commit adultery." She then asks for forgiveness and salvation.

The emotion-packed first poem is followed by a three-stanza dialogue between the soul and Jesus. Also written in first person, this rhyme expresses resignation. Yet it seeks to relieve uneasy feelings among the community by subtly shifting the burden of execution to Susanna herself. Thus, it changes "they will end my life" and begins, "Soon must I end my life" (*"Bald muß ich mein Leben enden"*). In a further attempt to overcome misgivings about the Cox execution, the poem feigns a happy ending by concluding, "And depart joyously from the world" (*"Und scheide froelich von der Welt"*). Likewise, the third and last poem begins with sentiments about letting go of life and ends with uplifting thoughts about finding joy and grace in Heaven.

By conveying a deep sensitivity to the tragic episode of Susanna Cox, these poems suggest a certain mood had settled among the populace at the time of her hanging. They reflect the profound dread and horror felt by the condemned—emotions seldom seen on Pennsylvania German broadsides concerning executions. Many broadsides dealing with executions, in fact, describe the outrageous deed perpetrated by the prisoner or they give no particulars at all. Most such broadsides are written in prose.

But broadsides containing ballads and other poems were exceedingly popular among Pennsylvania Germans. Most broadsides that contain lyrical verses degenerate into moralistic preaching, but unlike the prosaic versions relating horrifying misdeeds, the use of poetry was intended to elevate the subject, turning the attention from the deed itself to what readers could learn from the deed. *"Reime,"* however, breaks from this mold in that the verses actually portray feelings, not in a generic way, but specific to Susanna. For someone to so quickly pen these rhymes between the time that the date of execution was set and the time of the hanging indicates a passion about Susanna Cox that had probably been building, perhaps for months. The first poem especially expresses Susanna's emotions, ranging from horror to fear to profound regret. The second and third rhymes turn attention from Susanna to the emotions of the community. They attempt to leave a sense of hope for Susanna's salvation, easing the trauma for those feeling the guilt of ending a human life.

The *"Reime"* broadside was probably printed in small numbers and sold just before or on the day of the hanging. More than likely, Ritter was hesitant about printing too many copies of *"Reime,"* for it was possible at the last moment that Susanna's sentence would be commuted. To date, only two surviving copies of the *"Reime"* broadside are known to survive. No clear record of sales appears in the *Adler* accounts, called "day books" or "cash books," but it may have sold to individuals in cash transactions that required no bookkeeping. Ritter probably sold them at a discounted wholesale level to the author or Reading merchants, and they in turn would resell them at a retail price of six cents. The *Adler* day books show "songs" sold for four cents around the date of June 10, 1809. Taken literally, the reference to songs excludes the *"Reime"* broadside, which contained poems rather than songs.

The *Adler* day books reveal that stationers and owners of general merchandise stores throughout Reading flocked to the Ritter print shop on June 10 to purchase printed copies of Susanna Cox confessions and songs. Although the day books do not make it clear, perhaps the "songs" refer to a broadside containing the words to the penitence hymn sung just before the hanging. As discussed, it was customary at that time to sing a hymn of the condemned's choosing prior to executing a person. Such a broadside allowed onlookers unfamiliar with the words to sing along.

Contrary to popular belief, the "song" broadside issued on June 10 did not contain the famous Susanna Cox ballad. Composed after June 10, the celebrated ballad contains a verse concerning Susanna being bled following the hanging, but when Ritter's songs were circulated on June 10, she had not yet been executed.

Undoubtedly anticipating large crowds, Reading businessmen took advantage of what they correctly viewed would be swollen numbers of potential customers right out their front doors. Prior to the day of the hanging, Reading merchant Jacob K. Boyer advertised in the *Adler* more often than usual. Boyer owned and operated a store on Callowhill Street that carried a general line of merchandise and stationary supplies. On June 10, he purchased from Ritter six dozen German-language Cox confessions, four dozen English-language confessions, and two dozen songs. Later the same day, he bought three dozen more confessions. Benjamin Davies bought three dozen English-language and two dozen German-language confessions. Davies bought two dozen more confessions later in the day. Mathew Richards bought two dozen German and one dozen English confessions, as well as one dozen songs. William Stahle bought six dozen German and three dozen English confessions and two dozen songs early in the day, and later that day, he bought an additional three dozen confessions and three dozen songs. Also, on June 10, other individuals, including James and Abraham Addams, George Repplier, John Birkinbine, and John Rose, came to the *Adler* for bulk purchases of confessions and songs. They paid on average about eight and one-half cents for a confession and a little over four cents per song. Undoubtedly, these were resold for a higher price.

At minimum, 552 Susanna Cox confessions and 132 songs were bought on June 10. These sales recorded in the *Adler* day books mostly consisted of bulk purchases by retailers who paid on credit. (Days, weeks, and even months later, some merchants returned unsold copies for a refund or to clear their debt.) Probably, Ritter also sold an untold number of confessions and songs for cash, some at the retail level directly to individuals. It seems clear that many hundreds of sheets regarding Susanna Cox changed hands on the day she was "launched into eternity."

Unfortunately, the *Adler* day books provide no descriptions of the confession and song other than stating the confession was available in both German and English. Likely, the confessions were eight-page pamphlets. As noted, the songs possibly were single-sheet broadsides that contained the penitence hymn Susanna allegedly chose for the public to sing at her hanging.

The *Adler* day books clearly show the confessions were more expensive than the songs, suggesting they consisted of more than one sheet. Importantly, far more copies of the confession sold on June 10 than songs, causing today's scholars to puzzle over why more confessions did not survive. To date, only a partial photocopy of a German-language edition is known. Considering the fact that pamphlets and books generally survived in greater numbers than single-sheet broadsides, which were viewed as ephemera and meant to be read and tossed, scholars expect more confessions should exist.

Regardless, at the very time Susanna's life came to an end, her story came alive through the words of printers. Gottlob Jungman was not only Reading's first postmaster, he pioneered the first English-language newspaper in Reading when he printed *The Weekly Advertiser* in May 1796. In 1800, he entered into partnership with printer Carl Augustus Bruckman (ca.1763–1819) and they printed *The Weekly Advertiser* together until 1806, when they dissolved their partnership. In addition to a German-language newspaper, Jungman continued to print *The Weekly Advertiser* until 1816, when he moved to Kentucky.

During his time as a printer in Reading, Jungman encountered financial difficulties. Of interest, he purchased almanac calculations from Johann Friederich Schmidt, the Lutheran pastor at St. Michael's Church in Philadelphia. Schmidt complained to his oldest son that Jungman was delinquent in paying for his calculations. The pastor's son in whom Schmidt confided was, of course, none other than the Frederick Smith who defended Susanna Cox.

Conceivably, Jungman printed Cox confessions in addition to those printed by Ritter. Or perhaps some were printed by Carl Augustus Bruckman. After 1806, Bruckman moved to Allentown, Pennsylvania, where he continued to print. In the June 23, 1809, issue of his German-language newspaper, *Der Northampton Adverteiser, und Allentaun Gazette,* Bruckman published the confession of Susanna Cox on the front page. It remains unknown if Bruckman traveled to Reading to witness the execution, but if he did, he could have picked up a copy of the confession from his former partner, Gottlob Jungman, or from any Reading printer.

Throughout the early decades of the nineteenth century, plagiarism was common, and even accepted without question, so the confession could well have been printed simultaneously by several printers. But rather than printing the confession as a stand-alone pamphlet, Bruckman probably reached a broader audience when he published the confession in his newspaper. Thus, like ripples on a pond, the legendary story of Susanna Cox spread beyond Reading. Soon, the anonymously penned ballad gave printers more material for keeping her memory alive.

18

THE SAD, SAD SONG OF SUSANNA COX

And he who did this song compose
And earnestly did dictate,
Did all this misery behold,
Was near the judgment seat.

—"THE NEW MOURNFUL SONG OF SUSANNA COX"

For generations to come, the repeated printing of the broadside containing the ballad of Susanna Cox fixed her story within the memories of descendants of Pennsylvania Germans. The more than eighty documented editions were published throughout the nineteenth century and into the twentieth century. As is true of the majority of broadsides, most Cox broadsides lack imprints displaying the name and location of the printer, but it is certain many printers produced them. The last known edition was printed in 1964 for the Kutztown Folk Festival. A study is currently underway that examines the ballad of Susanna Cox broadsides from early letterpress printings, through lithographic editions, and into the period when inexpensive photocopies of earlier examples were distributed.

Renditions of the ballad, referred to by locals as the "Sad, Sad Song of Susanna Cox," usually consist of thirty-two stanzas, printed in two or three columns. The English-language examples are almost

always translations from the German rather than original composi-
tions. More than eighty percent of surviving Susanna Cox ballad
broadside editions are printed in German.

The German-language version of the ballad of Susanna Cox
was probably composed soon after her execution. It was printed
numerous times, followed by English translations as well as at least
one bilingual edition. Throughout the nineteenth century, the ballad was also printed in newspapers. According to a translation by
folklife scholar Don Yoder, additional lines on one unusual broadside say the ballad was first written on a barn door.

Often, broadsides concerning murders and executions had
graphic images, called "cuts," mostly showing coffins. The broadsides concerning the Moore and Charles executions, for example,
shows one coffin on one edition and two on another. Although
many Susanna Cox broadsides exhibit decorative borders, only
one edition discovered to date is known to have a cut. That edition
was printed by Thomas R. Weber (1818–89) of Hellertown, Pennsylvania, and includes a graphic with bars of music and children
playing musical instruments. Significantly, Cox broadsides invari-
ably show her name in large letters at the top. Thus, her name
alone became so familiar, it was sufficient for all to know the subject of the broadside.

To capture public attention, the headlines or subheads of Pennsylvania German broadsides dealing with murder frequently
described the crime as "gruesome." No known edition of the
Susanna Cox broadside uses the word gruesome in large type at
the top. Rather than focusing on the murder, the Cox ballad presents a sympathetic view toward the accused. For example, an
English-language version called "Tale of Sorrow" offers excuses for
what happened. One could even say it describes the extenuating
circumstances that were so glaringly absent at Susanna's trial. In
the "Tale of Sorrow," a stanza describes Susanna's upbringing. She
is portrayed as an innocent girl, reminding readers of Baum's
words that she was "as innocent as a child."

She had no knowledge of the world,
Took all for right she saw.

Knew nothing of the will of God,
Nor of the moral law.

Another stanza partially blames the baby's father.

As wedded man he lured her on,
And brought her deep disgrace.
But he must suffer for his crime,
In some dismal place.

Susanna Cox broadsides show the famous ballad in two main versions, each of which has several minor variations. One version includes the last name of the alleged father, Peter Mertz ("March" in some English-language editions), while the other does not. Most name Mertz in the fifth stanza.

An anonymously printed, German-language pamphlet of twelve pages contains what is believed to be the first printing of the ballad. Titled "A Newly Composed Song" ("*Ein Neu aufgesetztes Lied*"), this pamphlet has an imprint that says, "Printed in this year" ("*Gedruckt in diesem Jahr*"), probably meaning it was printed in 1809. The "Newly Composed Song" identified the father of the baby simply as "M." On June 13, 1809, printer Henrich Sage (pronounced Saga) published an article in the Lebanon paper, "*Der Weltbothe, und Libanoner Wochenschrift*," that revealed the father was "P-r M-z." Ten days later, on June 23, Carl Augustus Bruckman in Allentown published the initials as "P- M-," as did the printed pamphlet showing Susanna's confession. Just why the author of the "Newly Composed Song" used the "M." alone remains unknown. Perhaps the author attempted discretion, whereas Sage and Bruckman edged closer to identifying the father.

Of interest, the first line of the "Newly Composed Song" contains a typographical error. It reads, "*Ach merket auf ihr Mensechen all*" rather than "*Ach merket auf ihr Menschen all.*" Thus, the typesetter added an extra "e" in the German word, "*Menschen.*" Typographical errors were not unusual, but they suggest type was set in haste. Perhaps because plagiarism was common, the printer of the "Newly Composed Song" wanted to scoop his competitors before they copied and sold it. Or just as likely, the printer wanted to get the song to the public while the Cox story was still an item of lively discussion.

Significantly, most versions of the ballad say the author himself was present at the trial and that he attended the hanging. Scholars have debated the identity of that author for years. There are two candidates: John George Hohman (d. after 1846) and John Philip Gomber (1764–1822).

The earliest to venture a guess about the name of the author of the Susanna Cox ballad was Louis Richards, whose source was "Jacob Brown, an aged resident." Jacob Brown believed the author was John Philip Gomber, a schoolmaster in Bern Township, Berks County. Gomber had close ties to the *Adler*. He and his wife, Catharine Mayer Gomber, purchased numerous printed house blessings and *Taufscheine* (birth and baptismal certificates) from the *Adler*. They hand-colored these large sheets and sold them back to the *Adler*. The publisher then sold them at a higher price to itinerant scriveners, who distributed them throughout the countryside to families of Pennsylvania German heritage.

Unlike Jacob Brown and Louis Richards, author and folklife scholar Alfred L. Shoemaker believed John George Hohman composed the Susanna Cox ballad. In "The Disputed Authorship of the Susanna Cox Ballad," Shoemaker based his attribution on the fact that Gomber's name appears in the *Adler* account books as having purchased quantities of printed *Taufscheine*, but not ballads. Shoemaker wrote that Hohman, on the other hand, "had ballad after ballad printed." Don Yoder points out, however, that Hohman generally included his name on ballads he authored, and documented editions of the Susanna Cox ballad show no authorship.

Hohman immigrated to America in 1802 with his wife, Anna Catharine. Of necessity, the Hohmans indentured themselves to pay their passage. Anna Catharine was bound out east of the Delaware River in New Jersey and John George was bound out on the west side in Bucks County, Pennsylvania. Immediately after Hohman served his three-and-one-half-year indenture, he began having broadsides printed at the *Adler*. In 1805, he was charged

$9.50 for eight hundred sheets of songs. Probably overly optimistic about sales, he struggled to pay for them. He purchased them in May, but it was not until the end of September that he made a partial payment of $1.50. He also had a broadside concerning a murder printed in 1811. Regarding this broadside, Hohman composed only three stanzas, which were added to a previously published ballad. Between those dates, no broadside has surfaced that directly and conclusively links Susanna Cox to John George Hohman.

Like Gomber, Hohman purchased *Taufscheine* in bulk from the *Adler*. He seemed less successful than Gomber in selling them, for he purchased fewer quantities. Instead, Hohman turned to authoring books and broadsides and editing and publishing previously printed materials. Hohman even published popular ballads in his last book in 1846. Although he made no claim that he authored the text, Hohman included the ballad of Susanna Cox.

Hohman is best known for his powwow book, *Der Lang Verborgene Freund* (*The Long Lost Friend*), which was first published in Reading in 1819–20 by Carl Bruckman (d. 1828), son of Carl Augustus Bruckman. A form of folk medicine, powwowing was popular among Pennsylvania Germans, and Hohman's book became a huge success. Eventually, *Der Lang Verborgene Freund* was translated into English, and like the Susanna Cox ballad, it went through many printings and editions in German and English for decades to come. Seemingly, *Der Lang Verborgene Freund* might have provided Hohman a tidy income, but it appears that was not the case. Perhaps Hohman was a poor money manager, because he always seemed to be broke.

Many similarities in the lives of Gomber and Hohman contribute to the confusion over the authorship of the Susanna Cox ballad. Both Gomber and Hohman resided in or near Pricetown at times in their lives. (Gomber is buried there at the Dunker Meeting House.) Both men were associated with the *Adler*. Both attempted to supplement their incomes by selling *Taufscheine* and broadsides. And both were poor.

In 1815, Hohman was taxed in Alsace Township, near Reading, at only fifteen cents. By 1835 and 1836, his taxes were eight cents a year, and even these were partially forgiven because he was unable to pay. In "John George Hohman, Man of Many Parts," Wilbur H. Oda points out that this was a small sum compared to others taxed in the area. Oda suggests Hohman may have over-committed himself financially when he purchased property from Jacob K. Boyer, the Reading merchant who bought numerous Susanna Cox broadsides and confessions from the *Adler* on the day of the hanging. Hohman purchased a little more than three acres from Boyer in 1819, but by 1825, Sheriff Daniel Kerper seized Hohman's "goods and chattels, lands and tenements" in order to raise $52.50 that Hohman still owed Boyer. On Christmas Eve in 1825, Hohman's home was auctioned off for $90. According to Oda, Hohman seemed "in financial straits the greater part of his life."

As candidates for authorship, both Gomber and Hohman were capable of composing the words to a ballad. Hohman's broadsides illustrate his writing abilities. Gomber surely knew how to write a ballad as well, because as a schoolmaster, he was acquainted with music; ballads, after all, were meant to be sung. Schoolmasters in German-speaking communities were expected to teach music and many were organists at churches affiliated with the schools in which they taught.

The words to ballads were commonly penned for existing melodies, so there was no need for Gomber or Hohman to compose music. A handful of Susanna Cox broadside ballads exhibit a "melody line" below the subhead, giving the name of a tune familiar to most people of the time.

Differences between Gomber and Hohman hint at their personalities. As Oda and Yoder have pointed out, Hohman had numerous broadsides printed with his name on them. Perhaps Hohman believed his name would drum up business for future publications, thus showing a practical side to Hohman that appears to have failed him. Hohman firmly believed authors should not hide from the public—a somewhat courageous policy at the time, because authors and printers were subject to extremely severe criticism. For example, in 1799, a contingent of military officers flogged Jacob Schneider for not revealing his source concerning soldiers who roughed up local citizens protesting against a new tax law. And a year before, after Gottlob Jungman printed a "savage attack" against George D. Gerrish, co-founder of the *Adler*, Gerrish disappeared from the scene. Jungman accused Gerrish in print of having been a horse thief in Maryland, a serious charge that perhaps made Gerrish realize he had no stomach for the news business.

But unabashedly, Hohman wrote in defense of *Der Lang Verborgene Freund*, "I sell my books publicly, and not secretly, as other mystical works are sold." Conversely, Gomber appears more modest, or perhaps more timid. If he had broadsides printed, he preferred anonymity.

Using financial success as a yardstick, it might be said that Hohman's ambitions outdistanced his abilities. Other than that, little is known about Hohman's personality. Gomber is another matter. Contemporaries describe him as "middling bad," "not good," and "pretty low." Yet, if Gomber wrote the ballad of Susanna Cox, he apparently had a sensitive side that belies these negative opinions.

Obviously, it is possible neither Gomber nor Hohman wrote the ballad of Susanna Cox. For generations, anonymous Pennsylvania Germans composed ballads that appeared on broadsides. Some have suggested that Reverend Pauli, or his son, composed the ballad. That is certainly a possibility, but if either father or son put pen to paper concerning Susanna Cox, he probably would have written the three poems that appeared on the emotionally charged "*Reime*" broadside. Unless their hearts were made of stone, the Paulis' intimate familiarity with Susanna's woeful tale probably moved them to tears as they continuously tended to her spiritual and emotional needs.

Debates continue about the authorship of the ballad of Susanna Cox. Regardless, the anonymous composer created an enduring piece of Pennsylvania German literature. Called the "most popular ballad of Pennsylvania," it was memorized and sung in German well into the twentieth century. A 1962 Boston Museum of Fine Arts catalog description of the only known freehand-decorated Cox ballad mentions Mrs. Jane Masonheimer, "one of the best of the traditional Pennsylvania Dutch ballad singers," who sang from memory all thirty-two stanzas of the ballad in 1936.

In his book *The Pennsylvania German Broadside*, Don Yoder notes that in 1961, he recorded the singing in German of the entire ballad "by a Lehigh County farmer's wife of eighty-nine years, who was visiting the [Kutztown Folk] Festival from the Allentown area." According to Yoder, "She sang the ballad slowly and dolefully, and her performance took more than ten minutes." Today, such performances are rare, but they remain proof that the story of Susanna Cox is a mainstay in the Pennsylvania German culture.

19

ADVICE FROM THE DEAD TO THE LIVING

She faithfully admonish'd all,
Young Folks especially;
Oh! Let, said she, my dreadful fate
To you a warning be!

—"A NEW DIRGE CONTAINING THE HISTORY OF SUSANNA COX"

Broadsides and ballads were not the only venues for spreading the Susanna Cox story. It would be expected that after the jury passed its verdict, rumors about her guilt would subside, but this was not the case. In fact, Susanna Cox had hardly been buried when rumors about her alleged crime and execution swelled—rumors such as her "smiling countenance" and dramatically climbing a scaffold for the hanging.

Importantly, many people familiar with her story, such as Charles Hetrick, the current owner of what was the Schneider-Geehr farm, question Susanna's guilt. Upon hearing her name today, Pennsylvanians often react with sudden emotion. Barbara Breininger, wife of folk artist Lester Breininger, is typical when she exclaims without hesitation, "Susanna Cox was framed!" The late Carola Wessel, a German-language broadside scholar at Göttingan University, remarked, "What could she do? Her options were so limited!" Others express lingering regrets or shake their heads with sadness.

As the years pass, Susanna's tale becomes increasingly embellished, leaving modern historians with a mess of a legend. Inaccuracies about the story probably began with Susanna's printed confession, which was distributed on the day of the hanging and possibly the day before. Portions of the confession found their way into newspapers, such as an article that appeared in the Lebanon newspaper, *Weltbothe*, published on June 13, 1809, three days after the hanging. The article gave an account of the crime and stated facts about the hanging. As mentioned, it provided more complete initials of the father, "P-r M-z," from which the name of Peter Mertz emerged. Historians have no idea if any of these claims are true. In fact, portions of Susanna's confession, written in third person, probably resulted from "creative" writing.

Confessions were not always confessions of the condemned, but fabrications by printers who profited from them. Many were notoriously inaccurate. In *A Brief Guide to Broadsides*, Ken Gibb states that printers often repeated the same confession, changing only names and dates. In his book, *The Death Penalty: An American History*, Stuart Banner cites the unique, but telling, case of Indian Julian. Julian's 1733 hanging produced a broadside war, with each publisher claiming his broadside contained the "true" words from Indian Julian. The first printer claimed his broadside, "Poor Julleyoun's Warnings to Children and Servant," was published at Julian's wishes in front of two witnesses. Not to be outdone, the second publisher claimed his broadside, "Advice from the Dead to the Living," was also published as a result of Julian's wishes, this time in front of three witnesses. The third printer claimed his broadside, "The Last Speech and Dying Advice of Poor Julian," included a statement supposedly from Julian himself, which stated emphatically, "I do hereby utterly disown and disclaim all other Speeches, Papers or Declarations that may be printed in my Name."

One factor that suggests confessions were fabricated involves language. Frequently, the language of confessions is superior in terms of grammar, vocabulary, and diction to language the condemned normally used. This certainly holds true for Susanna's confession. She attended school for only three months, and her confession states, probably accurately, that she scarcely learned her alphabet. Yet, Susanna's confession was printed in English and in a formal and sophisticated style of High German rather than the dialect.

Obviously, someone recorded Susanna's confession on her behalf, raising the possibility that portions of the confession were fabricated. The members of the closely connected Schneider, Ritter, and Jungman families may have known the name of the father and imparted that information to the public, at least in the abbreviated form of "P-M-." But "P-M-" could represent many names. Hence, it is possible that "Peter Mertz" grew from rumor.

As fictionalized versions of the Cox tragedy developed, especially those printed during and after the 1880s, Susanna's age became an issue. She grew younger and younger, some newspapers claiming she was only sixteen. From both the Schwarzwald Reformed Church baptismal records and her confession, it is clear Susanna had just turned twenty-four at the time of the hanging. Perhaps presenting her in the papers as a cherub-faced youngster generated more sympathy from readers. It is also possible Susanna had been confused with the sixteen-year-old Mary Meloy. Whatever the reason behind the age discrepancy, Susanna's age can be stated with certainty—she was twenty-three when her infant was born and twenty-four when she was hanged.

Many later articles state that Susanna was attractive. Until eyewitness accounts were uncovered, her appearance remained a mystery. Authors making unsubstantiated claims about her age said she was pretty, but these sources obviously are deemed unreliable. Since eyewitness accounts have come to light, however, assessments can be made about her appearance. As noted, Jacob Bright Hoff's description of Susanna was found in Louis Richards's scrapbook. Hoff claimed she was indeed attractive with black hair and black eyes. Another interview found in the same scrapbook consists of a fragment of an article. The eyewitness's name is unknown, but he or she corroborates Hoff's testimony. Susanna was pretty.

In the court records, Jacob Geehr claimed Susanna's stout frame hid her pregnancy. Although Geehr said "large frame," Susanna probably was not tall. At the hanging, the rope was too short to reach the gallows and Susanna had to be elevated. From all accounts it can be concluded that she was short, somewhat heavy-set, but attractive. Mentions were also made of her ruddy complexion. The pink cheeks, however, may have resulted from the physical exertion of her walk to Gallows Hill. Contemporary newspaper accounts of the hanging report that June 10, 1809, was an unusually warm day.

Other factual information concerning Susanna's story has been distorted over time. Some articles of the late nineteenth century and early twentieth century—and one admittedly fictionalized account of the tragedy—claim the baby was six weeks old when murdered. While this makes for a more dramatic account, it is not true. The story is gripping enough and needs no embellishment.

The location where the baby's body was found frequently changed depending on the source. One account claims the body was found under a building. Another calls the washhouse the woodshed, and yet another describes the hole as a cave. Jacob Geehr clearly stated he found the body in a hole in the washhouse.

Some accounts say the three defense attorneys, Marks John Biddle, Charles Evans, and Frederick Smith, were paid with money raised by concerned citizens of Reading. Others add that Barbara Katzenmoyer led the campaign to raise these funds. This is yet another misconception. Courts maintained a small pool of lawyers to represent indigent defendants. In other words, they were early versions of the public defender. While defense attorneys possibly received compensation for their time, payments likely came from the borough rather than the individuals represented, at least in capital cases involving indigents. Their pay would have been a modest amount or only enough to cover expenses.

The ballad of Susanna Cox, itself, is the genesis of many rumors. One of the most obvious misconceptions comes from the stanza concerning the doctors trying to revive Susanna after the hanging. The following stanza is from Louis Storck's translation from the German:

> *Although without the least delay*
> *Their skill the doctors tried,*

To bring her back to life again
Was to their art denied.

This is yet another rumor that can be put to rest. As discussed previously, doctors did not attend executions to revive the condemned, even if they felt the doomed was unjustly executed. Instead, doctors were on hand to make sure the condemned actually died.

Furthermore, the ballad says Susanna implored young people witnessing the hanging to remain on the straight and narrow. While this portrays Susanna in a sympathetic light, records indicate she remained silent throughout the entire ordeal, save perhaps for singing the penitence hymn. Also, the Cox ballad states with certainty that a murder occurred, but the "murder," as previously noted, could have resulted from a tragically mishandled birth. Although the ballad, newspaper articles, and court records reflect the assumption of murder, doubt remains as to whether a crime was actually committed. In fact, the dislocated jaw and the blood in the throat are consistent with the theory that a difficult birth, perhaps followed by a frantic effort to resuscitate the infant, caused its death. In short, the biggest misconception of all in the Cox case was whether or not a crime was committed.

Whether related accurately or not, the Cox case strikes a familiar chord for generations before and after concerning the social issues of marriage and abandonment of parental responsibilities. Susanna is symbolic of many women caught in a similar situation. Today, she is viewed as having been trapped in social mores that proved exceedingly harsh. Over the years, many such women met unhappy endings. Yet, for Susanna's legend, there is no ending at all. Although romanticized versions of the Susanna Cox tragedy stray from the facts, they rekindle a fascination with her that never completely dies.

20

HER EXIT—INFAMY

Short was, and sad, her pilgrimage,
Her youth mere drudgery,
Her age but twenty years and four,
Her exit—Infamy.

—"A NEW DIRGE CONTAINING THE HISTORY OF SUSANNA COX"

Aside from the media coverage the Cox case received in June 1809 and beyond, another reason for the survival of the story can be attributed to various high-profile Pennsylvania murders throughout the years. In each of the murders, the death penalty was a real possibility. The newspapers, journalists, and citizens of Reading and southeastern Pennsylvania kept Susanna's tale alive to serve as an example of the consequences of murder, but also the collective uneasiness a community bears when someone is executed. Because so many still feel Susanna Cox was innocent, she serves as a reminder of the potential guilt that comes with terminating a life—albeit legally.

The story resurfaces time and again whenever a similar event occurs. Corresponding with the printing of Jacob Bright Hoff's eyewitness account of the Cox case was the 1881 trial and subsequent hanging of Catherine Miller in Pennsylvania. She and her paramour were convicted of killing Catherine's husband and were sentenced to death. Catherine was hanged in a prison on February 3, 1881.

In 1901, another gruesome murder was committed in the area. This time, John Edwards was the victim. His wife, Kate, and her black lover, Samuel Greason, were charged for the crime. After a protracted trial and extensive newspaper coverage, both Greason and Edwards were sentenced to death. At first, each of the parties claimed the other did it, but as the time of death drew nearer, Edwards claimed the murder was hers alone. The case caught the public's attention largely because of the Edwards children. Many sympathetic accounts mentioned the youngest child visiting Edwards in prison. While in prison, Edwards gave birth to yet another child, this one belonging to Samuel Greason. As the case was being dissected by journalists, the Cox legend was again resurrected. Journalists and laypersons alike drew comparisons between the two cases. As with any controversial subject, some wrote in favor of capital punishment and others cited the Cox case from the standpoint of abolishing the death penalty. Upon Edwards claiming the murder was hers alone, Greason was released from death row. Kate Edwards escaped Susanna's fate as well. After receiving a recommendation from the Board of Pardons, Gov. Samuel Pennypacker withdrew the death warrant. Once the Edwards murder was resolved, the Cox story dwindled again in the news.

In 1900, Richards wrote his article, "Susanna Cox: Her Crime and its Expiation," a paper from which so many accounts draw information. Soon after, in 1905, Susanna's bones were allegedly discovered during the widening of Hampden Boulevard, again thrusting her into public view. As with her baby, no record was kept as to what happened to her bones. More than likely they were reinterred in a potter's field. But murders and skeletons were not the only events that renewed interest in Susanna Cox.

In 1965, officials at the Kutztown Folk Festival began hanging Susanna Cox in effigy. Although the configuration of the gallows is inaccurate (for safety and theatrical reasons), her legend takes center stage. Overall, the story told at the festival is true. Susanna has since been hanged annually for more than forty years.

In history books about Reading and Berks County, whether it is Philip E. Pendleton's *Oley Valley Heritage*, Morton L. Montgomery's *History of Berks County*, George and Gloria Jean Meiser's *The Pass-*

ing Scene, Raymond W. Albright's *Two Centuries of Reading, Pennsylvania,* or Irene Reed's *Berks County Women in History,* the Cox story resurfaces. Her story even appears in books about social issues such as Marvin Olasky's *Abortion Rites: A Social History of Abortion in America.* In addition to books, numerous articles tell the tale of Susanna Cox, such as Wayne E. Homan's "The Sorrow Song of Susanna Cox" or Kenneth Sell's "P. Pauli: Prisoner, Professor, Preacher." Although no stone memorials were erected for Susanna Cox in Reading's City Park, perhaps for fear of vindicating a murderess, she is arguably one of the best-remembered women who ever lived in Berks County.

In 1994, a movie was made about the case, *The Ballad of Susanna Cox,* starring Mary W. Hedahl. Some information the producers supplied for the newspapers promoting the film proved factual. For example, a chronology provided to newspapers followed events accurately. As is typical in historical films, many details were fictionalized as an obvious attempt to dramatize the story. The film had a small production budget and limited circulation. Some who saw it were less than thrilled with the results. A pastor at a local church in Reading became alarmed that the film portrayed Reverend Pauli as something of a buffoon. Inaccurate details in the film include the following: Susanna had an abortion and the trial was a cover-up for this act; Susanna and her family were Irish; Barbara Katzenmoyer rallied the community on Susanna's behalf; Susanna's mother forcibly made Susanna's father, whose first name is incorrect in the film, watch the hanging; Barbara ran to and sobbed over Susanna's body and made the officials remove the death hood; and most absurd, the spectators commented, "That was a fine hanging." The movie also suggests that Susanna was raped. That is a possibility, but it is the more probable she was seduced. Because no man claimed responsibility, it can be concluded the father of Cox's infant was of questionable moral character. Today, some call him an out-and-out coward.

The film was but one telling of the Cox story within the realm of current performing arts. A play was commissioned in 2007 by Eric Schaeffer, artistic director of Signature Theatre in Arlington, Virginia. The play *Nest* was written by Bathsheba Doran. According to an online account about the play, Schaeffer was influenced by the Kutztown reenactment of Susanna's hanging and thought her legend would be a fitting piece for the theater to perform. The play makes less of a claim concerning the truth. Instead, it is based on the legend of Susanna Cox, not her life story. In the play, Susanna was portrayed as a Mennonite indentured to a well-educated, childless couple named Jacob and "Elizabeth" Geehr. Many other variables occur in the fictionalized play.

According to a review of *Nest* written by Karen Alenier, Susanna Cox seems contemporary. At one point, when Jacob bemoans the fact that the character Elizabeth is barren, Susanna points out that Geehr may be the problem, not Elizabeth. Apparently, some writers believe this modernization of Susanna Cox would appeal more to contemporary viewers. As recently as 2009, *Nest* was performed at the University of California–Davis. Of interest, Doran felt the ballad was essential to the Cox legend and a portion of the play is devoted to it.

Beyond traditional means of storytelling, Susanna Cox is portrayed in other mediums. For example, the band Those Galloping Hordes pays tribute to the saga. The band is comprised of three talented members, all of whom grew up in or near Berks County. Corey Higman, Tyler Long, and Danny Mink play a variety of instruments. While the band began as a duet when Higman and Mink performed together at the Kutztown Folk Festival, the three collaborated to create a "dedication to the story of Susanna Cox, which might possibly be the saddest point in Berks County History." Their musical scores are named after characters or events related to Susanna Cox, such as "Mr. Jacob Geehr" or "Tow or Flax." The band is currently recording a full-length compact disc devoted to the Susanna Cox story.

Abbreviated versions of the legend appear on the Internet. In an undated article titled "Pennsylvania German Legends," Adam Kirchhoff notes the ballad claims Susanna was seduced by the married man, not the other way around. Often, unwanted pregnancies are blamed on "loose" or naively flirtatious women. Kirchhoff observes that as early as 1809, the ballad suggests the father was the main culprit in the seduction.

A new generation is showing an interest in Susanna Cox. An entertaining article begins, "Did you know that Northeast is haunted? . . . Her name is Susanna Cox, and her story is a gruesome and sad one. We warn you, if you are easily upset, stop now!" In 2008, "Ghost of Northeast Middle School—Fact or Fiction?" was researched by two students for their school newsletter, *The Panther Pause*. Rachel Dreibilbis and Rebecca Shuker of Northeast Middle School in Reading wrote the article because Cox's ghost purportedly haunts the school premises, causing odd happenings that disrupt studies. According to the authors, Susanna has favorite spots to haunt, including the first floor and the fourth floor. Like Charles Hetrick, the girls credit a search for justice as Susanna's main motivation. They also wonder if Susanna is perhaps searching for her infant. The authors believe Susanna's grave is somewhere beneath the school, perhaps the gym. Their article even contains a picture of what may be Susanna's ghost. A teacher supports the young authors' research, revealing that many of the older teachers have talked about the haunting through the years, especially when the gym was being built.

Just as Susanna Cox was an "invisible" member of society from the date of her baptism in 1785 until her tragic end, evidence of her existence has vanished. As mentioned, the original trial notes are missing and Frederick Smith's copious records show a blank page where notes about the case should appear. Only the cellar remains of the washhouse. Of the confession, only a partial photocopy is known. And her bones disappeared after 1905. But history has not erased Susanna Cox's story. The ballad carried her legend into the twentieth century, and the Kutztown Folk Festival reenactment keeps her story alive today.

Perhaps the 1809 court record will reappear someday. These musty pages may shed new light on the story. Meanwhile, articles about Susanna Cox continue to pepper newspapers and the Internet. And now this book, by relating as much truth as is currently known, is dedicated to helping separate fact from fiction regarding the legend of Susanna Cox.

The lesson from the Cox story is that societies that judge their members, as most societies do, should approach with caution those actions that could taint their narrative. Through the fog of two hundred years, history will never know if Susanna Cox murdered her newborn. A newspaper article from the late nineteenth century called "Hurriedly Hanged" reflects the attitude of many regarding the execution. The anonymous author summed up the feelings of many familiar with her legend when he said, "Of all the executions that have ever taken place in eastern Pennsylvania, that of Susannah Cox will always stand out as the most hasty, interesting, and possibly the most undeserved on record."

BACK TO THE FESTIVAL

Let all who live upon this earth,
. By her example see,
What dire disgrace may those befall
Who're raised illiterately.

—"A NEW DIRGE CONTAINING THE HISTORY OF SUSANNA COX"

While conducting research for this book, the authors had the opportunity to visit the Schneider–Geehr farm. Charles Hetrick, the current owner, is the third generation of his family to operate the property. On a cold January day, nearly two hundred years after the discovery of the infant's body, Hetrick and his daughter took time from their work to give us a tour.

After walking through the farm with its sad yet unforgettable history, we were in need of a break to gather our thoughts, so we dined at the familiar old Yellow House Hotel, near Douglassville, not far from Susanna's place of birth. We wanted to keep our impressions of the area intact, and there was no better way than to dine in the former home of Peter Nagle Jr. Today, the Yellow House Hotel advertises, "Getaways are getting harder to find, but amidst the hustle and bustle of modern life, there are still a few old-style pleasures within quick and easy reach."

After the excursion to the Yellow House Hotel, we walked City Park, where Susanna was hanged. The park's beautiful, grass-covered hills overlook the city of Reading, keeping secret its once sinister past. One can imagine the citizens of today's Reading flocking to the park, never guessing that two hundred years ago a life was ended there on a warm day in June.

Like Berks County, the Kutztown Folk Festival never fails to delight. According to a 2007 news release, festival representatives are questioned every year regarding the appropriateness of the reenactment of the Susanna Cox hanging. They point out that it is a historic event, part of the Pennsylvania German culture that they are representing. While anxious feelings towards the reenactment are understandable, this and other terrible events have haunted our nation's past. While tragic, some of these incidents have brought about change for the better.

The reenactment serves as a small reminder, amid the wonder at the festival, that our ancestors were human and imperfect. In 1809, they wrestled with controversies concerning crime and punishment. To their credit, they examined all sides of the issue. Many came to realize Susanna Cox was caught in a struggle between time-honored tradition and enlightenment concerning what constituted justice. Without considering the pros and cons of capital punishment, if nothing else, the Cox story demonstrates that every person in this country matters. Her story drives home America's ideal that our legal system should protect everyone.

In a small way, Susanna Cox and her baby helped shape a nation. Their deaths were not in vain, because they effected change. Citizens examined the cause and effect of criminal behavior and its consequences. They abandoned antiquated precedents brought from the Old World. Specifically, Susanna's hanging brought an end to executing women in public in Pennsylvania. Eventually, all public executions were stopped in the commonwealth, which proved time and again to be progressive in matters of crime and punishment.

After Susanna's execution, courtroom protocol became more stringent and developed into practices we recognize today. Today, an appeals system is in place and no stone is left unturned for protecting defendants. "Innocent until proven guilty" is not only a standard, but a crucial part of our legal system. In short, laws protect citizens as opposed to protecting the status quo. Concern regarding Susanna Cox's death played a small role in these developments, because it was often cited by those demanding change.

While watching the effigy of Susanna swing on a warm summer day in Kutztown, we could not help but think of the quiver of the gallows on a similar day two hundred years before. In 2008, the rope shudders and groans as it takes the jarring weight of the mannequin. Even in this age of movies, television, and desensitization to violence, the sight of that life-sized doll plummeting through space elicits gasps of horror from the audience. The final words of the somber narrator, "Her exit—Infamy," reverberate throughout the otherwise quiet corner of the festival. The audience hesitates, as if uncertain whether to applaud June DeTurk's poetic narrative, for by doing so they also applaud Susanna Cox's hanging. Most clap softly, respectfully.

In 2008, we recalled the written record of one who witnessed the hanging—the young Jacob Pile. On the afternoon of June 10, probably in 1875, he was at the train depot in Pottstown, Pennsylvania, waiting for a train. He struck up a casual conversation with a fellow traveler by saying it was the anniversary of Susanna Cox's execution. Obviously familiar with the Cox story, the stranger quietly asked Pile, "Is it right?"

Pile, at this point an attorney, responded, "It is the law."

The person asked again, "Yes, but is it right?"

Pile responded, "I think she might have been pardoned."

BIBLIOGRAPHY

Albright, Raymond W. *Two Centuries of Reading, Pa., 1748–1948: A History of the County Seat of Berks County.* Reading, PA: Historical Society of Berks County, 1948.

Banner, Stuart. *The Death Penalty: An American History.* Cambridge, MA: Harvard University Press, 2002.

Crosby, Molly Caldwell. *The American Plague: The Untold Story of Yellow Fever, the Epidemic That Shaped Our History.* New York: Berkley Publishing Group, 2007.

Drimmer, Frederick. *Until You Are Dead: The Book of Executions in America.* New York: Carol Publishing Group, 1992.

Earnest, Russell, and Corinne Earnest. *Flying-Leaves and One-Sheets: Pennsylvania German Broadsides, Fraktur, and Their Printers.* New Castle, DE: Oak Knoll Books, 2005.

Friedman, Lawrence M. *A History of American Law.* New York: Simon & Schuster, 2005.

Gibb, Ken. "A Brief Guide to Broadsides." 2008. http://johnjohnson.wordpress .com. Retrieved 7 August 2009.

Meiser, George M., and Gloria Jean Meiser. *The Passing Scene.* Vol. 15. Reading, PA: Historical Society of Berks County, 2007.

Montgomery, Morton L. *1748–1898 History of Reading, Pennsylvania.* Reading, PA: Times Book Print, 1898.

———. *History of Berks County in Pennsylvania.* Philadelphia: Everts, Peck & Richards, 1886.

———. *Historical and Biographical Annals of Berks County Pennsylvania.* Chicago: J. H. Beers & Company, 1909.

Nolan, J. Bennett. *The Smith Family of Pennsylvania.* Self-published by the Smith family, 1932.

Oda, Wilbur H. "John George Homan, Man of Many Parts." *The Pennsylvania Dutchman* 1, no. 16 (18 August 1949): 1.

Pendleton, Philip E. *Oley Valley Heritage: The Colonial Years: 1700–1775.* Kutztown, PA: The Pennsylvania German Society, 1994.

Pennsylvania Archives. Third Series, vol. 18. Harrisburg, PA, 1897.

"Philadelphia Society for Alleviating the Miseries of Public Prisons," Pennsylvania Prison Society Records (collection 1946). Historical Society of Pennsylvania.

Ramsland, Katherine. *Beating the Devil's Game: A History of Forensic Science and Criminal Investigation.* New York: Berkley Publishing Group, 2007.

Richards, Louis. "A Vanished Landmark—The Old County Jail" [paper read before the Historical Society of Berks County], 13 December 1910.

———. "Susanna Cox: Her Crime and its Expiation" [paper read before the Historical Society of Berks County], 13 March 1900.

Riordan, Liam. *Many Identities, One Nation: The Revolution and Its Legacy in the Mid-Atlantic.* Philadelphia: University of Pennsylvania Press, 2007.

Schwartz, Bernard. *The American Heritage History of the Law in America.* New York: American Heritage Publishing Company, 1974.

Sell, Kenneth D. "P. Pauli: Prisoner, Professor, Preacher." *Journal of the Johannes Schwalm Historical Association* 3, no. 2 (1986): 16–21.

Shoemaker, Alfred L. "The Disputed Authorship of the Susanna Cox Ballad." *The Pennsylvania Dutchman* 1, no. 2 (12 May 1949): 1.

Shoemaker, Henry W. *The Black Moose in Pennsylvania.* Altoona, PA: Altoona Tribune Company, 1917.

Snyder, David Geise. "Dr. Bodo Otto: Physician to Washington's Army," *Drumbeat* 25, no. 3 (Autumn 2007): 11–13.

Teeters, Negley K. *Hang by the Neck: The Legal Use of Scaffold and Noose, Gibbet, Stake, and Firing Squad from Colonial Times to the Present.* Springfield, IL: Charles C. Thomas, 1967.

Yoder, Don. *The Pennsylvania German Broadside: A History and Guide.* University Park, PA: Pennsylvania State University Press, 2005.

ACKNOWLEDGMENTS

This book was written with the support and encouragement of many people. We especially thank Dr. Don Yoder, a true mentor and friend, for his enthusiasm concerning our project. We were delighted and honored he offered to write the foreword.

Special recognition goes to our editor, Kyle Weaver of Stackpole Books. Kyle facilitated our progress at every step of the way.

Lester and Barbara Breininger, who not only make history but live it, went beyond the pale to share with us. As a Pennsylvania Dutchman and folk artist, Lester has knowledge of the "Dutch" culture that amounts to far more than turning mud into redware.

We are grateful to Philip E. Pendleton, author of *Oley Valley Heritage: The Colonial Years*, for sharing knowledge about that part of Berks County, Pennsylvania, where the Susanna Cox story began.

The Historical Society of Berks County in Reading has been essential to many of our past and present endeavors. Regarding the Susanna Cox project, thanks goes to Kimberly Richards, Director of Special Collections; Joshua Blay, Museum Curator; and Ellen Sloan, Librarian and Archival Assistant. We also thank the society's volunteers, Miles and Betty Dechant, Evans Goodling, Donna Humbert, Judith Merkel, Irwin Rathman, and Ruth Shaffer.

A mainstay in all our studies is the Pennsylvania State Archives in Harrisburg. Head of References Services Jonathan R. Stayer, Dr. Amanda Weimer, and Brett Reigh consistently aim us in the right direction.

A general note of gratitude goes to the staff and volunteers at the Historical Society of Pennsylvania in Philadelphia and the University of Delaware Morris Library in Newark, Delaware. Also, the staff at the Dover, Delaware Public Library, particularly Librarian Maria Bunce and Consumer Health Librarian Patty Hartmannsgruber, deserve special recognition.

At the Kutztown Folk Festival, Dave Fooks, Executive Director, and Pattie Boyer, Administrative Director, provided helpful background about the festival.

The staff and students of Northeast Middle School in Reading played a unique part in our Susanna Cox story. As such, we thank Principal Alex Brown, teacher Stephanie Adam, and promising journalists Rachel Dreibilbis and Rebecca Shuker.

Our personal thanks goes to Corinne Dempsey, who greeted us with hot coffee and words of encouragement at our many breakfast meetings at the local restaurant.

The following individuals were also instrumental in telling the story of Susanna Cox:

Jerome Abrams, M.D., of Dover, Delaware; Lorraine Bell, Archivist and Historian, First United Church of Christ in Reading, Pennsylvania; Rev. Richard R. Berg of the Lancaster Theological Seminary in Lancaster, Pennsylvania; Julie M. Choma, Collections Manager, Philip and Muriel Berman Museum of Art at Ursinus College, Collegeville, Pennsylvania; Patricia DeGrazia, Proprietor, Yellow House Hotel, Yellow House, Pennsylvania; June DeTurk, narrator, Kutztown Folk Festival; Rev. Mark D. Dewald, First United Church of Christ in Reading, Pennsylvania; David and Karen Hampel, Lansdowne, Pennsylvania; Charles Hetrick, Berks County, Pennsylvania; Heather Deppen Hillard, Research Analyst, Pennsylvania House of Representatives, House Archives, Harrisburg, Pennsylvania; Gary Johnson, Newspaper and Current Periodical Room of the Library of Congress, Washington, D.C.; Lucy Kern, Librarian, Pennsylvania German Cultural Heritage Association, Kutztown, Pennsylvania; Albert C. King, New Brunswick, New Jersey; Michael Lear, Archivist, Franklin and Marshall College, Lancaster, Pennsylvania; Ken Leininger, Denver, Pennsylvania; Andrew Lloyd, Professor of Microbiology at Delaware State University, Dover, Delaware; Debbie Louie, Forensic Chemist, Delaware State Police, Dover, Delaware; Roxanne MacAnnany, artist, Delaware; Susan Mazza, Bureau of State Library, Harrisburg, Pennsylvania; Daniel Mink and Those Galloping Hordes, Berks County, Pennsylvania; Hunt Schenkel, Archivist, Schwenkfelder Library and Heritage Center, Pennsburg, Pennsylvania; Kevin Shue, Genealogist, Lancaster County Historical Society, Lancaster, Pennsylvania; Diane Skorina, Reference Librarian, Myrin Library, Ursinus College, Collegeville, Pennsylvania; Kevin Spangenberg, Bureau of State Library, Harrisburg, Pennsylvania; Elizabeth Sustello, Berks County, Pennsylvania; Eric Suter, Research Assistant, Dover, Delaware; Larry Ward, Reading, Pennsylvania; Carolyn Wenger, Curator, Lancaster Mennonite Historical Society, Lancaster, Pennsylvania; Michael Whitehead, Archivist, Archival and Records Management Services, County of Berks, Leesport, Pennsylvania; and Darryl Wonderly, Hamilton, New York.

Finally, a study of Susanna Cox could not have been written without the contributions of Louis Richards (1842–1924). Richards was a Berks Countian who served in the Civil War, then became a lawyer, journalist, and historian. He was president of the Historical Society of Berks County from 1902 to 1917. His article, "Susanna Cox: Her Crime and its Expiation," and his handwritten transcriptions of the Susanna Cox trial notes were critical to our research.

INDEX